ANTI-INDECENCY GROUPS AND THE FEDERAL COMMUNICATIONS COMMISSION

ANTI-INDECENCY GROUPS AND THE FEDERAL COMMUNICATIONS COMMISSION

A Study in the Politics of Broadcast Regulation

Kimberly Zarkin

Mellen Studies in Journalism
Volume 3

The Edwin Mellen Press
Lewiston•Queenston•Lampeter

Library of Congress Cataloging-in-Publication Data

Zarkin, Kimberly.
Anti-indecency groups and the Federal Communications Commission : a study in the politics of broadcast regulation / Kimberly Zarkin.
p. cm. -- (Mellen studies in journalism ; v. 3)
Includes bibliographical references and index.
ISBN 0-7734-6761-0 (hardback)
1. Broadcasting--Law and legislation--United States. 2. Obscenity (Law)--United States. 3. Broadcasting policy--United States. 4. American Family Association. 5. Morality in Media, Inc. 6. United States. Federal Communications Commission. I. Title. II. Series.

KF2805.Z37 2003
343.7309'94--dc21

2003046339

This is volume 3 in the continuing series
Mellen Studies in Journalism
Volume 3 ISBN 0-7734-6761-0
MSJ Series ISBN 0-7734-7143-X

A CIP catalog record for this book is available from the British Library

Front cover photo courtesy of Kimberly Zarkin
Author photo courtesy of Lowrance Photography

The Edwin Mellen Press
Box 450
Lewiston, New York
USA 14092-0450

The Edwin Mellen Press
Box 67
Queenston, Ontario
CANADA L0S 1L0

The Edwin Mellen Press, Ltd.
Lampeter, Ceredigion, Wales
UNITED KINGDOM SA48 8LT

Printed in the United States of America

To my grandfather, Robert Fernald,
my father, Peter Dalianis,
and my husband, Michael Zarkin:
The three people who mean home to me.

Table of Contents

Preface i

Acknowledgements ix

Chapter One: Introduction 1

Theoretical Framework 2

Statement of the Problem and Research Questions 4

Methodology 8

Outline 11

Chapter Two: Review Of The Literature 13

Indecency 13
Historical 14
Constitutional 17
Unique Looks at Indecency 20

Citizen Groups at the FCC 23

Krasnow, Longley, and Terry 29

Summary of the Literature 32

Chapter Three: The History Of Indecency Regulation 35

Early Attempts at Regulation 36

Defining the Parameters 41

The Supreme Court Decision and the Aftermath 47

The April 1987 Trio 49

The Battle Over the Safe Harbor....51

Fines and Settlement....55

Summary....60

Chapter Four: Morality In Media And The American Family Association....63

Morality In Media....63
Pornography and Other Concerns....64
Broadcast Indecency....68

American Family Association....71
Pornography and Other Concerns....74
Broadcast Indecency....80

Summary....82

Chapter Five: Research Findings: Evidence Of American Family Association And Morality In Media Influence On Indecency Regulation....85

Complaint Files....85

Blocking Renewals and Acquisitions....92

Lobbying and Ex Parte Communication....94

Notices of Inquiry and Notices of Proposed Rulemaking....98
NOI on Broadcast Indecency, Docket 89-494....99
NPRM on Broadcast Indecency, Docket 92-223....105

Nomination Hearings....106

Oversight Hearings....110

Summary....111

Chapter Six: Analysis And Conclusions....113

Complaint Files....113

Blocking Renewals and Acquisitions....116

Lobbying and Ex Parte Communication....119

Notices of Inquiry and Notices of Proposed Rulemaking....120

Congressional Hearings....122

Krasnow, Longley, and Terry's Model of the Broadcast Policy-Making System....123

Why Do Citizen Groups Fail? 125
Suggestions for Further Research 127

References 129

Document Reference List 151

Index 157

Preface

In the volume you hold in your hand Kimberly Zarkin reviews the efforts of the American Family Association and Morality in Media to affect the Federal Communications Commission's attempts at the regulation of indecency. In the process, she dispels a myth–at least as far as radio-TV is concerned: the supposed inevitable success of the religious right in pushing their agenda.

Both American Family Association (AFA) and Morality in Media (MIM) are citizen groups. As this book goes to press the heyday of citizen group activism in broadcasting is some three decades in the past. In that time the radio-TV business has changed radically: competition has multiplied, but mergers and buyouts have reduced the number of different owners. Many consumers do not realize that there is a difference between, say, the local NBC-TV affiliate and the USA network, other than the specific programs they schedule. Regulatory thinking has been turned upside down: FCC members, law makers and jurists routinely assume that scarcity is no longer a factor, and regulators have even suggested that broadcasters be granted property rights to the frequencies they use. The FCC has eliminated regulatory vehicles that citizen groups used in the past; license renewals, for example, are now almost automatic, and the commission has done away with the fairness doctrine. Nonetheless, even today a careful scanning of the trade press can occasionally reveal the existence of a citizen group attempting to buck current trends and influence the shape or content of broadcasting.

The origins of the citizen group are tied to the very nature of broadcasting. For years the only radio-TV programming in existence came by way of over-the-air–no cable, no VCRs, no DVDs, no World Wide Web, no SMATV systems, no VOD. And "over the air" was strictly terrestrial–no digital satellite transmission, no wireless cable. So if you wanted to listen to a particular radio station, you turned on a radio capable of receiving radio broadcast stations over the air and tuned it to that station. If you wanted to watch a particular TV station, you turned on a television receiver attached to an antenna and tuned it to that station. Your receiver would then pick up the station and reproduce its programming–assuming, of course, that your receiver was in the coverage area of the station's signal.

That was called *broadcasting*, and it utilized *radio waves* to distribute programming. Radio waves are part of the electromagnetic spectrum, which also includes (among other forms of radiation) visible light. Each station uses a group of waves (or "frequencies") in which to carry its programming; this is the station's *channel.* Like light, radio waves are natural resources and not subject to private ownership. As such, they are said to be *in the public domain.*

There are a finite number of channels available for broadcasting, and because of the potential for interference, any given channel can be used only once in a particular area. This means that radio waves are not only natural resources; they are *scarce* natural resources. This is the *scarcity factor*, and contrary to popular myth, it does still exist. Try, for example, to operate two AM radio stations in the same town, both transmitting on the same channel of, say, 850 kHz. The signals of the two stations would interfere with each other, and listeners would hear two different programs at once, unintelligible gabble. Because of the scarcity factor, broadcasting is different from most other forms of mass communication. The number of book publishing firms, magazines, daily newspapers and motion picture studios and theaters you start in a town, for example, is limited only by the amount of money you have to invest. On the other hand, if you want to start a broadcast station there's a good chance that all frequencies have already been taken, some by local stations, some by stations in the next town, some by stations hundreds of miles away but still subject to interference.

Since only a limited number of people can broadcast at any given time, that brings up the question of how to choose those people. Early on federal courts determined that broadcasting is a form of interstate commerce, and so Congress, acting under its Constitutional mandate to regulate interstate commerce, wrote the relevant laws in 1927 and 1934. The result was establishment of an appointed agency (named the Federal Communications Commission in the latter act), one of whose jobs was to choose which applicants would be licensed to operate broadcast stations. The laws also provided a criterion for the agency to use in making that choice: before granting or renewing a broadcast license the commission was first to determine that the *public interest* would be served by that grant or renewal.

Ironically, for 39 years the public–you and I–had almost no say in determining whether grant of a broadcast license would serve the public interest. The FCC asserted that only other licensees who demonstrated an economic stake in a license proceeding could participate in the case. A local TV station gives an unfair, one-sided presentation of controversial issues in your town? Too bad; there was nothing *you* could do about it . . . until the mid-1960s. That was when Federal Appeals Court decisions established the right of the public to participate in the licensing process. This touched off formation of citizen groups, groups of individuals who had no monetary investment in radio or television transmission facilities but who felt that, as citizens, they should have some say over the actual transmissions themselves, transmissions that, after all, utilized those scarce natural resources in the public domain. Citizen groups challenged station license renewals, and, the FCC adopted rules whose net effect was to encourage the public to take a more active interest in renewal proceedings.

About the same time, citizens began to file fairness doctrine complaints about commercials and other aspects of broadcast programming. According to a 1949 FCC statement, a broadcast licensee whose station aired one side of a controversial public issue had to ensure that the other side was presented, too; this was the *fairness doctrine*. In the late 1960s citizen groups attempted to use this requirement in a variety of situations and, thus, expand the types of issues to which the fairness doctrine applied.

Citizen groups now had the power to force broadcasters to listen to them, and they used it. This was the high point of citizen activism. Stations entered into negotiations with the groups, discussing policies, soliciting suggestions and making agreements. Some groups functioned on the national level, taking note of research that showed increasing evidence of links between exposure to televised violence and aggressive behavior in the viewer. They worked to curb a trend in prime-time programming toward gratuitous sex and violence. They used publicity, complaints to the FCC and meetings with network officials. Most groups were main stream in nature, representing the broad, middle ground of American thinking–e.g., United Church of Christ, American Medical Association, the PTA–as well some organizations formed for the specific purpose of dealing with broadcasters, such as Action for Children's Television. The important thing here, however, is not who these groups were, the tactics they used nor even the goals of their efforts; it is the model they established: *citizen groups pressuring broadcasters and regulators to change, require or restrict programming.* The model, of course, was not limited to main stream groups.

Religious organizations and leaders had long used broadcasting to extend the reach of their services and theological bent. During the 1970s, however, Christian evangelists turned to television to reach audiences. They packaged video ministries in slick, often star-studded productions and paid stations to carry them. Their audiences were small but intensely loyal. Audience contributions financed not only the programs but also ancillary organizations such as colleges, broadcast stations and theme parks. Most television evangelists professed fundamentalist theology and conservative social values. Some took advantage of a trend toward political conservatism and "born-again" faith that swept the country to increase their influence. They played active roles in politics and claimed credit for helping elect Ronald Reagan and other conservatives into public office. They also joined an increasing number of voices that called for broadcasters to clean up their programming.

Not all religious-based activist groups were fronted by big-name evangelists. But all used the model of citizen activism, and so all became well-known to the broadcasters and regulators at which they aimed their efforts. Two of the most prominent were Morality in Media and American Family Association. Both were launched by relative "unknowns," and both focused much of their effort on the elimination of indecency from the airwaves.

Indecent is a common term, but when used in the context of broadcast programming and regulation it has a special and somewhat arcane meaning. The courts have determined that First Amendment rights do not protect *obscene* material. There are, of course, some words and other material that, while not legally obscene, are not the type of thing to which we want our children (and perhaps even ourselves) exposed. But since such material does not meet the legal definition of obscenity, government may not suppress it. On the other hand, if such material is broadcast; then it may be indecent, and the FCC can take action to forbid it. Confusing, to say the least, but Zarkin sorts it out and reviews the legal evolution of the concept of indecency.

Zarkin's study focuses on *policy*, anything government does or does not do to solve a public problem. MIM and AFA saw broadcast indecency as a public problem, and they used the avenues open to citizen groups to pursue their goal: elimination of indecent material from the air waves. The primary question this research seeks to answer has to do with the groups' impact on policy: did MIM and AFA affect FCC policymaking and, if so, how? Certainly one feature that makes this study worthwhile is that it demonstrates the religious right does not always get what it wants. As shown herein, AFA and MIM were successful only when their aims and goals happened to coincide with those of the policy makers–e.g., the FCC or Congress. One might assume Reagan-era office holders, grateful for the help they supposedly received from MIM, AFA and the like would push the groups' media policy agenda. The reality, however, is that the office holders did not do much to advance that agenda.

A second feature of this study that makes it worthwhile is Zarkin's use of the prevailing model of broadcast policymaking. That use works two ways: the model helps to explain and to validate her findings, and her well-researched case study, in turn, helps to support the model.

A third worthwhile feature is the very fact that the information reported herein has been assembled and interpreted. This information has never before been put together and published in a single document.

But there is more, much more in these pages, not the least of which is the information provided on the groups themselves–how and why they formed, their leadership, their aims, their tactics. It is a worthwhile effort and an interesting read.

Les Smith, Professor
Department of Telecommunication
University of Florida

Acknowledgments

Books are never written by just one person. The work you hold in your hand could not have been completed without a lifetime of dedication from my family, teachers, friends, and strangers who performed random acts of kindness. I owe a debt of gratitude to more people than I can name. But here, I offer my thanks to some who contributed most directly.

My doctoral committee at the University of Florida: Milagros Rivera-Sanchez, F. Leslie Smith, Bill F. Chamberlin, Albert Matheny, and Ken Wald deserve many thanks. Scholars are not born -- they can only be created through the loving dedication of their teachers.

Thomas Winkler, Ginny Simms, and Sandra Watson at the FCC guided me through the bureaucracy, gave me access to the files I needed, and answered my questions with a graciousness above and beyond the call of duty.

The staff at the Government Documents room of the University of Florida library found me many a dusty volume of Congressional hearings.

The faculty and staff at Texas Woman's University and La Salle University gave me a place to be a teacher and scholar and the courage to hope this work would someday be more then just a computer file.

Finally, my husband, Michael Zarkin, without whom I'd drown in doubts and empty pizza boxes.

Chapter 1
Introduction

The regulation of indecent language on the broadcast airwaves has been a controversial issue, raising significant First Amendment concerns since the beginning of broadcasting itself.[1] Determining what material is indecent and when, if ever, that material should be broadcast is largely the province of the Federal Communications Commission (FCC). But the FCC is an agency that is often described as particularly open to outside influences, as pointed out by Krasnow, Longley, and Terry in their seminal book, The Politics of Broadcast Regulation.[2]

One of the sources of influence that Krasnow, Longley, and Terry discuss is citizen groups. On matters of broadcast indecency, those groups have generally been conservative religious organizations such as Morality in Media (MIM) and the American Family Association (AFA). These anti-indecency groups have long been active in attempting to influence the FCC's actions regarding the broadcast of indecent material. But questions about the constitutionality of the regulations,[3] as

---

[1]Milagros Rivera-Sanchez, "Developing an Indecency Standard: The Federal Communications Commission and the Regulation of Offensive Speech, 1927-1964," Journalism History 20:1 (1994): 3-14 and Milagros Rivera-Sanchez, "The Regulatory History of Broadcast Indecency, 1907-1987" (Ph.D. Diss., University of Florida, 1993).

[2] Erwin G. Krasnow, Lawrence D. Longley and Herbert A. Terry, The Politics of Broadcast Regulation (New York: St. Martin's Press, 1982), 304.

[3] For example, see Daniel L. Brenner, "Censoring the Airwaves: The Supreme Court's Pacifica decision," in Free But Regulated: Conflicting Traditions in Media Law, ed. D. L. Brenner and W. L. Rivers (Ames, IA: Iowa State University Press, 1982), 175-180; Paul J. Feldman, "The FCC and Regulation of Broadcast Indecency: Is There a National Broadcast Standard in the Audience?"

well as allegations of selective enforcement,[4] have complicated the issue. Because of the murkiness surrounding the regulation of indecency, a clear understanding of all the players in the policy-making process is relevant.

By examining the activities of Morality in Media and the American Family Association as related to the FCC, this research attempts to provide a clear picture of whether these groups have had any impact on the policy-making process. Anecdotally, evidence of the impact exists. But since no scholar has attempted to document comprehensively that impact, this research fills an important gap in the understanding of how the FCC has regulated indecent speech on the broadcast spectrum as well as how it has responded to the pressure of interest groups. In addition, this research may also give scholars further insight on how the FCC makes policy in general. The key to finding this understanding is the theoretical framework provided by Krasnow, Longley, and Terry in The Politics of Broadcast Regulation.

Theoretical Framework

In The Politics of Broadcast Regulation, the authors present a theoretical framework that describes the complexities inherent in the government's attempts to regulate broadcasting. Their framework is a model designed to aid in understanding the political process rather than acting as a predictive agent.[5] The significance of the model, while a simplified view of the world, is that it "directs attention to, and focuses it on, key relationships and activities, and, by doing so,

---

Federal Communications Law Journal 41:3 (1990): 369-400; Jay A. Gayoso, "The FCC's Regulation of Broadcast Indecency: A Broadened Approach for Removing Immorality from the Airwaves," University of Miami Law Review 43 (1989): 871-919; and Helene T. Schrier, "A Solution to Indecency on the Airwaves," Federal Communication Law Journal 41:1 (1990): 69-107.

[4] Seth T. Goldsamt, "'Crucified by the FCC'? Howard Stern, the FCC, and Selective Prosecution," Columbia Journal of Law and Social Problems 28 (1995): 203.

[5] Krasnow, Longley, and Terry, 74.

helps define order in the multiple phenomena of the subtleties of the real political world."[6] Understanding the ways in which anti-indecency groups interact with other regulatory actors and impact the process of regulating broadcasting is the purpose of this study. The Krasnow, Longley, and Terry model is the best theoretical framework available.

According to the authors, two of the reasons the regulation of broadcasting is so problematic are statutory ambiguities and recurring controversies.[7] The regulation of broadcast indecency involves both. Section 326 of the Communications Act of 1934[8] says "[n]othing in this Act shall be understood . . . to give the Commission the power of censorship over the radio communications . . . and no regulation or condition shall be promulgated . . . which shall interfere with the right of free speech by means of radio communication."[9] On the other hand, Section 1464 of Title 18 of the United States Code makes it a federal crime to broadcast "any obscene, indecent, or profane language by means of radio communication."[10] This statutory contradiction is the root of much of the controversy over the regulation of broadcast indecency.

The regulation of broadcast indecency is also an issue that is recurring. Since the beginning of broadcasting, the efforts to maintain "decency" on the broadcast spectrum have waxed and waned, but never completely disappeared. Because the regulation of broadcast indecency involves several of the problems that Krasnow, Longley, and Terry see with the regulation of broadcasting as a whole, like statutory ambiguity, this issue is well suited to the framework they present.

---

[6] Krasnow, Longley, and Terry, 74.
[7] Krasnow, Longley, and Terry, 18.
[8] This section, along with §1464 of Title 18 of the US Code, originated in the Radio Act of 1927.
[9] 47 U.S.C. § 326.
[10] 18 U.S.C. § 1464.

In the model, there are six major participants in the regulatory policy-making process. The three core actors are the FCC, Congress, and the broadcast industry. The other three principals are the White House, the courts, and citizen groups. The role of these latter three actors, while significant, is usually far less immediate and direct than the previous three.[11] It is the relationships between these six players that make up Krasnow, Longley, and Terry's model. The FCC, being the primary regulatory agency, is the focal point of the model. The industry and Congress provide the other points on an outer triangle. The courts, citizen groups, and the White House are the points on the inner triangle, showing their lesser influence in the process. Each of the six points is connected by channels of varying significance that illustrate how these players may affect each other in the policy-making process. This research uses this model to attempt to understand how MIM and AFA might have influenced the course of indecency regulation.

Statement of the Problem and Research Questions

Attempts at regulating indecent language on the broadcast airwaves has been around for nearly as long as broadcasting itself.[12] Despite this lengthy history, the research on the regulation of broadcast indecency is incomplete. The forces behind the regulation remain, for the most part, unexplained. The purpose of this research is to fill in some of those gaps.

Because Section 1464 of Title 18 of the United States Code makes it a federal crime to broadcast "any obscene, indecent, or profane language by means of radio communication,"[13] one of the core issues in the regulation of broadcast speech is the distinction among obscene, indecent, and profane language. The definitions provided below lay out the legal distinctions among these terms.

[11] Krasnow, Longley, and Terry, 75.
[12] Rivera-Sanchez, "Developing an Indecency," 3-14.

Obscenity is illegal in this country, one of the few types of speech not protected by the First Amendment to the Constitution. While the fact that it is illegal is rarely debated by the judicial community, the definition of what is obscene has always been controversial. The current legal definition of obscenity comes from the 1973 Supreme Court decision, Miller v. California.[14] In Miller, the Court established a three-part test to determine whether material was obscene:

> (a) whether the average person, applying contemporary community standards would find that the work, taken as a whole, appeals to the prurient interest; (b) whether the work depicts or describes, in a patently offensive way, sexual conduct specifically defined by the applicable state law; and (c) whether the work, taken as a whole, lacks serious literary, artistic, political, or scientific value.[15]

As a legal term, indecency is most commonly associated with broadcasting. According to a 1975 FCC Order, broadcast indecency is defined as material that "describes in terms patently offensive to contemporary community standards for the broadcast medium, sexual or excretory activities or organs, at times of the day when there is a reasonable risk that children may be in the audience."[16]

Although much of the language is borrowed from the Miller definition of obscenity, there are some differences. For example, material is not obscene if, taken as a whole, it has serious literary, artistic, political, or scientific value. A broadcast, on the other hand, can be found indecent based on a single excerpt. In addition, that a broadcast has literary, artistic, political, or scientific value does not mean is it *per se* not indecent.

The most important difference is that while obscenity is not protected by the First Amendment, indecency is. The Supreme Court found in FCC v. Pacifica in 1978 that broadcast indecency could be regulated, however, because of the

---

[13] 18 U.S.C. § 1464.
[14] 413 U.S. 15 (1973).
[15] 413 U.S. 15, 25.

technological characteristics of television and radio, including its accessibility to children. The history of the regulation of indecency on broadcasting is presented in depth in Chapter 3.

Despite the inclusion of profanity in section 1464, profane language is generally outside the purview of FCC regulation. Profanity is defined by Black's Law Dictionary as "irreverence towards sacred things" or "vulgar, irreverent, or coarse language."[17]

While past scholarship on the regulation of broadcast indecency has reviewed the actions of the FCC, the courts, and Congress, little attention has been paid to how the citizen groups have affected those government organizations and their positions on the regulation of broadcast indecency. The purpose of this study is to answer the following question: What impact have the American Family Association and Morality in Media had on government attempts to regulate indecent speech on the broadcast airwaves? By measuring this impact, further understanding can be gained regarding how the government goes about regulating speech.

This study is limited in that it does not address all of the citizen groups that have played a role in the regulation of indecency. Instead, the American Family Association and Morality in Media were chosen as representative of those groups. Both are national in scope. Morality in Media was founded in 1968 and the American Family Association, beginning as the National Federation for Decency, was founded in 1977. These two groups, while both politically and socially conservative religious organizations, do differ somewhat in their methods of lobbying the government on the issue of the regulation of indecency.

---

[16] 56 FCC.2d 94.
[17] Black's Law Dictionary (St. Paul, MN: West Publishing Company, 1979), 1087.

Primary among these differences is what some political scientists call "insider" and "outsider" strategies.[18] When discussing administrative agencies, insider strategies involve utilizing many of the same tactics as the regulated industry, such as formal comments and personal lobbying of staff. A group using the outsider approach, however, tends to avoid the traditional channels of communication and takes a more grassroots approach. These groups may use direct communication from the public to the decision makers, rather than the more personal, insider approach.

Morality in Media takes the more formal, legal approach. The group files formal comments with the FCC as a means to change policy. It has also utilized other means of access, including the submission of amicus briefs to the courts, and drafting legislation. This represents insider strategy; MIM often approaches the Commission much like a member of industry or some other actor who is active in attempting to influence policy.

The American Family Association, while also active in submitting complaints and comments to the FCC, focuses most of its attention on outsider activity: advertisers, boycotts, and training its members to monitor stations for indecent broadcasts. AFA is an example of a group that uses channels of communication to the Commission that are not commonly used by other regulatory actors.

These differences in strategy, as well as the length of existence of the two groups, were key reasons for focusing on the American Family Association and Morality in Media.

---

[18] See, for example Jeffrey M. Berry. Lobbying for the People (Princeton, NJ: Princeton University Press, 1977); and Allan J. Cigler and Burdett A. Loomis, eds. Interest Group Politics, 3rd ed. (Washington, D.C.: Congressional Quarterly Press, 1991).

This study is also limited in that it does not include all the players in the Krasnow, Longley, and Terry model. Instead, it focuses solely on the core of the Krasnow, Longley, and Terry model: the FCC. While the citizen groups in question may have used other avenues of influence, like the Congress and the courts, to affect the regulation of indecency, the scope of this research does not allow for the exploration of these venues. That is something for a future study.

Methodology

This study relies primarily on legal and historical research methods. While political influence is largely mercurial and fleeting, a paper trail suggesting influence by these citizen groups does exist. Evidence was found by searching documents both published by and filed with the FCC and Congress. This research examines six areas of possible influence. Four are areas where the groups had direct contact with the FCC, including complaint files, challenges to renewals and acquisitions, lobbying, and the formal comment process for Notices of Inquiry and Proposed Rule-Making. The other two areas of possible influence involve group activity through Congress, specifically testifying at nomination and oversight hearings.

The research presented here was gathered from a number of sources. Some of the material came from the published records of the FCC and Congress. Both paper and electronic resources such as the LEXIS-NEXIS database and the Congressional Masterfile Index CD-ROM were used to locate the appropriate information in the FCC Record, the Congressional Record, and Congressional Committee Reports.

The information on the complaints that have been sent to the FCC came from the files of the Complaints and Compliance Office of the Mass Media Bureau's Enforcement Division. Current files and those closed files that are less than seven years old are accessible to the public at the Complaints and Compliance Office in Washington, D.C. Some older files were examined at the Washington National Records Center in Suitland, Maryland.

A search of the FCC database in LEXIS provided the information for the sections on the petitions to deny license renewals or transfers. That research also provided some of the information for the lobbying section. The LEXIS search turned up twenty-seven mentions in the FCC Record of Morality in Media.[19] Of those twenty-seven records, only those involving broadcast indecency directly were used in this research. A search for material relating to the American Family Association[20] turned up 967 entries. Almost 99% of those mentions involve AFA's actions in front of the Commission as a licensee.[21] The handful of those not involving AFA's stations that did touch upon broadcast indecency were used in this research.

Other material for the lobbying/ex parte section came from a variety of sources. Media coverage of the groups' actions was one source. Information was also drawn from copies of letters sent between the FCC and AFA and MIM as well as copies of a few appointment calendars and Commission memos.[22]

The material from the dockets, the comments and reply comments, used in this research is available in the FCC Public Reference Room. The contents of docket 92-223 are available through the FCC's Record Image Processing System.[23] The contents of docket 89-494 are kept in binders at the Reference Room. It

---

[19] The FCC Record Database (FEDCOM/FCC) was searched with the phrase "Morality in Media."

[20] The FCC Record Database (FEDCOM/FCC) was searched using "American Family Association," "Wildmon," "National Federation for Decency," "Coalition for Better Television," and "Christian Leaders for Responsible Television." Only "American Family Association," "Wildmon," and "National Federation for Decency" were present in the Record.

[21] AFA owns a number of stations and translators across the country.

[22] This material was originally gathered by through a Freedom of Information Act request made by Crigler and Byrnes for their article, "Decency Redux: The Curious History of the New FCC Broadcast Indecency Policy."

appears that the record of docket 92-223 is complete. However, docket 89-494 is incomplete. The Report of the Commission stated that the FCC had received 92,500 formal and informal responses to the Notice of Inquiry.[24] The material available in the Reference Room is contained in four large binders. The binders contain all of the formal comments listed in the FCC's report, but only a handful of the informal comments. No one at the FCC knows the location of the rest of the docket.

The information on the group's attempts to influence the FCC through Congressional hearings came mainly from the Congressional Masterfile. Searches were performed to locate all of the nomination hearings from 1961 until 1994. Those hearings were read for evidence of any involvement by the American Family Association and Morality in Media. Another search of the CMI database provided the list of all the times that the groups participated in other, non-nomination related, Congressional hearings over the years.

Another method that might have aided this research was interviews with the participants in the policy process. Unfortunately, many of the key players in the regulation of indecency were not readily available. People like Mark Fowler, Jack Smith, and Alfred Sikes could not be reached. In addition, the composition of the staff at the FCC has changed over the years, thus making it difficult to trace those staff members who participated in the process unreachable as well. Current FCC staff in the complaints and compliance office were interviewed, but little of pertinence to the research was found.

---

[23] This a an electronic storage system for comments filed with the FCC.
[24] 5 FCC Rcd 5297, 5297 (1990).

Outline

This study attempts to find whether the American Family Association and Morality in Media had an impact on the regulation of broadcast indecency.

Chapter 2 is a review of the relevant literature. Research on the regulation of indecency, the role of citizen groups at the FCC, and work that utilizes or critiques the Krasnow, Longley, and Terry model are presented.

Chapter 3 outlines the history of indecency regulation from the 1962 decision in the Palmetto Broadcasting case to the end of the tenure of Reed Hundt as chair of the FCC. This time span was chosen because the 1962 Palmetto decision marks the beginning of the current era of the regulation of indecency. And since the chair sets the agenda of the Commission, the departure of Chairman Reed Hundt in 1997 is an opportune endpoint.

Chapter 4 provides the history and stated goals of Morality in Media and the American Family Association. Particular attention is paid to the tactics and resources that these groups brought to bear in their fight against broadcast indecency. This information comes from both the organizations themselves and media coverage of the groups.

Chapter 5 is devoted to discussing any evidence of influence that these groups had at the FCC. Among the areas that are considered are complaint files and Notices of Proposed Rule-Making.

Chapter 6 is the summary of findings and the analysis. This chapter also examines the findings in the context of the Krasnow, Longley and Terry model. In addition, this chapter also presents an evaluation of why citizen groups have historically found little success in changing Commission policy.

Chapter 2
Review Of The Literature

The regulation of indecency is a topic that has not been ignored by the academic community; nor is the role of citizen groups at the FCC untouched ground. But the combination of the two, linked with the Krasnow, Longley, and Terry model, is largely unturned soil. This literature review covers these three areas to show the need for this research. First, the existing literature on the topic of indecency is reviewed. Second, the literature on citizen groups at the FCC is examined. Finally, research that has used the Krasnow, Longley, and Terry model is considered.

Indecency

A review of the literature shows that indecency research falls into two main categories. One is historical, where the emphasis is on description rather than analysis. Another area of the literature is the constitutional analysis. In this research, authors have sought to prove that the policy itself, or how it has been enforced, is a violation of the First Amendment of the constitution. A small number of articles do not fit into these divisions and are presented at the end of this section.

Historical

Many authors have written extensive, and sometimes exhaustive, histories of the regulation of indecency. These descriptive articles served an important scholarly purpose in documenting what has happened through the years. Many of these articles and books have concluded that the regulation of indecency is really nothing more than a guessing game, and that while vague patterns do exist, there are no hard and fast rules.

One grouping of the historical research on indecency focuses solely on a single event. These articles present the facts, but rarely place the events in a larger context. In a 1979 article called "The Charlie Walker Case," broadcast historian F. Leslie Smith delved into the FCC's records and media reports from the time to describe the events surrounding the revocation of the license of Palmetto Broadcasting.[1] This historical look at an early effort to remove explicit material from the airwaves presented the facts admirably but did not place the events within a political context. The same holds true for another in-depth piece about a later event in the history of indecency. "The Rise and Fall of Topless Radio," written by John C. Carlin in 1976, looked only at the short-lived and successful campaign by the FCC to get the sexually explicit radio shows off the airwaves.[2] Although this was a politically-charged time, Carlin did not attempt to do much more than present the facts.

Another grouping of the historical research on indecency is the projects that cover years of regulation rather than a single incident. In some cases, these are chapters within books about broadcasting in general. For example, both Lucas Powe and William Ray include sections on the regulation of indecency in their respective works. Powe's book American Broadcasting and the First Amendment

---

[1] F. Leslie Smith, "The Charlie Walker Case," Journal of Broadcasting 23:2 (1979): 137-151.

includes a chapter entitled "Maintaining Cultural Morality."[3] In that chapter, he provides the historical facts of the regulation of indecency covering more than twenty years. In addition, his personal commentary and perspective is woven throughout the chapter. He portrays the regulation as a cultural battle tied tightly to the political and social upheaval of the 1960s and 1970s. Despite the attempts to fit the regulation into the larger, cultural landscape, Powe never places the regulatory history in a policy framework. Similarly, William Ray's account of life in the FCC, The Ups and Downs of Radio Regulation, describes what happened in the course of the regulation of indecency and includes some details, particularly of political agendas, that are not published elsewhere.[4] But Ray, like Powe, never discusses a wider policy framework.

The final grouping of historical research to be presented here is the work of media law scholar Milagros Rivera-Sanchez. Beginning with her 1993 doctoral dissertation, The Regulatory History of Broadcast Indecency, 1907-1987,[5] Rivera-Sanchez has sought to discern patterns in the regulation of indecency. To this end, she has examined the regulation in more detail than any other scholar. Her research traces the development of the definition of indecency back to the beginning of broadcasting itself,[6] using documents from the FRC and FCC, Congress, the courts, and both the trade and popular press. Even with this exhaustive research, Rivera-Sanchez could find no clear patterns in the early

---

[2] John C. Carlin, "The Rise and Fall of Topless Radio," Journal of Communication Winter (1976): 31-37.
[3] Lucas A. Powe, Jr. 1987. American Broadcasting and the First Amendment. Berkeley: University of California Press.
[4] William B. Ray, FCC: The Ups and Downs of Radio-TV Regulation (Ames: Iowa State University Press, 1990), 193.
[5] Milagros Rivera-Sanchez, "The Regulatory History of Broadcast Indecency, 1907-1987" (Ph.D. Diss., University of Florida, 1993). See also Milagros Rivera-Sanchez, "Developing an Indecency Standard: The Federal Communications Commission and the Regulation of Offensive Speech, 1927-1964," Journalism History 20:1 (1994): 3-14.
[6] Most scholars begin in the 1960s.

history of the regulation of indecency. And, like other authors, she did not present the information within a policy framework.

In more recent articles, Rivera-Sanchez has again attempted to find patterns in the FCC's actions, this time in the last ten years. Two of the articles mirror each other, two halves of the search to determine exactly what the FCC means when it says something is indecent. The first, "How Far is Too Far? The Line Between 'Offensive' and 'Indecent' Speech"[7] investigated indecency complaints that had been dismissed by the Commission. The second, a co-authored piece with Michelle Ballard, is "A Decade of Indecency Enforcement: A Study of How the FCC Assesses Indecency Fines (1987-1997)."[8] This article looks at the broadcasts that have resulted in fines. These articles focus on the content of the broadcasts that listeners complained about. From this information, the authors attempt to reach a conclusion about how the Commission goes about defining indecency. The result of the research is only the barest of frameworks; the only strong conclusion Rivera-Sanchez could reach is that if the Commission had fined something once, it most definitely would fine the same material again.

In another co-authored piece by Ballard and Rivera-Sanchez, "Settlement: FCC's Newest Strategy to Address Indecency?"[9] the authors discuss the settlements reached by the FCC with two broadcasters who had racked up considerable fines for indecency. While the authors determine that the settlement was a political decision, the analysis goes no further and does not explore the policy ramifications of the Commission's actions.

---

[7] Milagros Rivera-Sanchez, "How Far is Too Far? The Line Between 'Offensive' and 'Indecent' Speech," Federal Communications Law Journal 49:2 (1997): 327-366.

[8] Milagros Rivera-Sanchez and Michelle Ballard, "A Decade of Indecency Enforcement: A Study of How the FCC Assesses Indecency Fines (1987-1997)," Journalism Quarterly 75:1 (1998): 143-153.

[9] Michelle Ballard and Milagros Rivera-Sanchez, "Settlement: FCC's Newest Strategy to Address Indecency?," Communications and the Law 18:4 (1996): 1-27.

A final type of historical research in the area of indecency is represented by two law review articles that delve into some of the politics behind the 1987 expansion of the regulation of indecency. In "Consistency Over Time: The FCC's Indecency Rerun,"[10] an article published in 1988, Lucas Powe returns to the topic of indecency to evaluate the April Trio cases in light of the history of the regulation. He tries to place the cases in political, legal and sociological context and concludes that the changes were simply consistent with the past. He views the cases as merely an attempt to relieve external pressure on the Commission. The source of that pressure is discussed in depth by John Crigler and William J. Byrnes in "Decency Redux: The Curious History of the New FCC Broadcast Indecency Policy."[11] That 1989 article looks, more than any other piece discussed thus far, at the politics that surround the regulation of indecency. Despite this attention to pressure on the Commission, neither piece places the events in a policy model that attempts to further understand the workings of the Commission.

Constitutional

Many articles present the regulation of indecency from a historical perspective. Many more, particularly in the law journals, look at the topic as a constitutional issue. Authors examine the history of indecency to find constitutional flaws that may or may not invalidate the regulation. Some authors look at the FCC's policy in general. Other research focuses on a single issue or comparison between cases or issues. In general, the authors conclude that the policy, no matter which way it is looked at, is unconstitutional.

---

[10] Lucas A. Powe, Jr., "Consistency Over Time: The FCC's Indecency Rerun," Hastings Comm/Ent Law Journal 10 (1988): 571-577.
[11] John Crigler and William J. Byrnes, "Decency Redux: The Curious History of the New FCC Broadcast Indecency Policy," Catholic University Law Review 38:Winter (1989): 329-363.

One way that authors have looked at the indecency rules in a constitutional light is to question the definition of the term indecent. For example, Daniel Brenner focused particularly on the decision in FCC v. Pacifica and determined that the Supreme Court was wrong in deciding that the Commission's definition of indecency was constitutional.[12] Other research, such as Helene Schier's "A Solution to Indecency on the Airwaves," agrees with the Supreme Court's position in Pacifica that indecency should be regulated, but questions the constitutionality of the later applications of the policy. Several authors, like Jeremy Lipschultz, Jonathan Weinberg, and Susan Wing look at the applications of the indecency policy over the years and conclude that the term indecent is so vague and overbroad as to be unconstitutional.[13] Jay Gayoso went further to conclude that this vagueness has led to pervasive chill on broadcasters.[14]

Two articles, "Children, Indecency and the Perils of Broadcasting: The 'Scared Straight' Case" by Harvey Jassem and Theodore L. Glasser[15] and "Obscene/Indecent Programming: Regulation of Ambiguity" by Charles Feldman and Stanley Tickton,[16] use comparison of broadcasts to reach a conclusion about the constitutionality of indecency regulation. The Jassem and Glasser piece contrasts the ruling in WBAI (Pacifica), that banned indecency from the airwaves

[12] Daniel L. Brenner, "Censoring the Airwaves: The Supreme Court's Pacifica decision," in Free But Regulated: Conflicting Traditions in Media Law, ed. D. L. Brenner and W. L. Rivers (Ames, IA: Iowa State University Press, 1982), 175-180.

[13] Jeremy Harris Lipschultz, "Conceptual Problems of Broadcast Indecency Policy and Application " Communications and the Law June (1992): 3-29; Jonathan Weinberg, "Vagueness and Indecency," Villanova Sports and Entertainment Law Forum 3 (1996): 221; and Susan Wing, "Morality and Broadcasting: FCC Control of 'Indecent' Material Following *Pacifica*," Federal Communications Law Journal 31:1 (1978): 145-173.

[14] Jay A. Gayoso, "The FCC's Regulation of Broadcast Indecency: A Broadened Approach for Removing Immorality from the Airwaves," University of Miami Law Review 43 (1989): 871-919.

[15] Harvey Jassem and Theodore L. Glasser, "Children, Indecency and the Perils of Broadcasting: The 'Scared Straight' Case," Journalism Quarterly 60:3 (1983): 509-512.

[16] Charles Feldman and Stanley Tickton, "Obscene/Indecent Programming: Regulation of Ambiguity," Journal of Broadcasting 20:2 (1976): 273-281.

unless late at night, to a broadcast of a documentary called "Scared Straight." This documentary was about life in prison and aimed at keeping adolescents out of trouble. It contained just about all the seven dirty words and was aired as early as 6:30 p.m. in some markets.[17] Despite the commonalties between the broadcasts, the "100 to 150 complaints" received by the FCC,[18] and the fact that the documentary was aimed at viewers under 18, the broadcast of "Scared Straight" resulted in no fines. This led the authors to conclude that the indecency rules were arbitrary and capricious. Similarly, the Feldman and Tickton article compares the decisions in Sonderling (topless radio) and Pacifica (WBAI) and, likewise, found that there was no consistency in the policy.

Another way authors have addressed the constitutionality issues is discussing a single aspect in depth. By focusing on one topic, the authors question whether the indecency regulations in general pass constitutional muster. For example, another Glasser and Jassem article looked at the Supreme Court's determination that indecent broadcasts are an unconstitutional intrusion into the privacy of the home.[19] In "'Crucified by the FCC'? Howard Stern, the FCC, and Selective Prosecution," Seth Goldsamt focused on the FCC's actions against Howard Stern as unconstitutional because of the uneven enforcement of the regulation.[20] In other research, both Wade Kerrigan and First Amendment scholar C. Edwin Baker examined the constitutionality of the safe harbor and found it lacking.[21]

---

[17] Many stations broadcast the documentary at 10pm, but Jassem and Glasser, 512 report that at least a dozen stations broadcast it at 8 or 9pm.

[18] Jassem and Glasser, 511.

[19] Theodore L. Glasser and Harvey Jassem, "Indecent Broadcasts and the Listener's Right of Privacy," Journal of Broadcasting 24:3 (1980): 285-299.

[20] Seth T. Goldsamt, ""Crucified by the FCC"? Howard Stern, the FCC, and Selective Prosecution," Columbia Journal of Law and Social Problems 28 (1995): 203.

[21] Wade Kerrigan, "NOTE: FCC Regulation of the Radio Industry: A Safe Harbor for Indecent Programming?," Iowa Law Review 79 (1993): 143; and C. Edwin Baker, "The Evening Hours During Pacifica Standard Time," Villanova Sports and Entertainment Law Forum 3 (1996): 45.

A major area of constitutional concern is the parameters of the community standards that are used to judge whether material is indecent. Obscenity laws began with national standards but as the definition of obscenity evolved in the Supreme Court, the Justices concluded that a local standard is the only constitutional way of judging what material is unacceptable. The FCC has determined, however, that the community standards specified in the indecency rule refer to a national standard for the broadcast audience. Several researchers disagree. A 1990 article by Paul Feldman concluded that the use of the national standard for indecency contravened years of constitutional precedent.[22] Similarly, when Jan Samoriski, John L. Huffman, and Denise M. Trauth developed a framework for indecency regulation, they determined that a local standard decided by a jury trial was the only constitutional way to determine whether a broadcast was indecent.[23]

Unique Looks at Indecency

A smattering of articles do not fit into the historical or constitutional views of indecency regulation. They look at the topic in unique ways, considering issues that few others have considered. There are three loosely grouped categories of this literature. The first concerns the courts and the regulation of indecency. The second deals with indecency and children. The final loose categorization is that of articles discussing reactions to indecency regulation.

While hardly an article is published that does not, in some way, critique the FCC, only a few focus on the courts as part of the regulatory process. Several

---

[22] Paul J. Feldman, "The FCC and Regulation of Broadcast Indecency: Is There a National Broadcast Standard in the Audience?," Federal Communications Law Journal 41:3 (1990): 369-400.

[23] Jan H. Samoriski, John L. Huffman and Denise M. Trauth, "Indecency, the Federal Communications Commission, and the Post-Sikes Era: A Framework for Regulation," Journal of Broadcasting & Electronic Media 39 (1995): 51-72.

articles that do not fit into the historical or constitutional categories place the judiciary at center stage. James Wesolowski's "Obscene, Indecent, or Profane Broadcast Language as Construed by the Federal Courts" focuses on the courts' attempts to define the terms obscene, indecent, and profane.[24] Likewise, John Huffman and Denise Trauth examine the Rehnquist Court's actions regarding obscenity and indecency for their consistency with its other rulings.[25] Both these articles interpret court decisions to reach their conclusions. On the other hand, Jeremy Lipschultz, in "The Influence of the United States Court of Appeals for the District of Columbia Circuit on Broadcast Indecency Policy," looks at the courts as playing an active role in the development of indecency regulation rather than simply ruling on definitional issues or following precedents.[26]

Another grouping of indecency articles focuses on indecency and children. This is an important topic, because the FCC's justification for the regulation of indecency is that children must be protected from this material. In "On the Regulation of Broadcast Indecency to Protect Children," Edward Donnerstein, Barbara Wilson, and Daniel Linz question the validity of that concern. After searching the relevant literature, the authors conclude that the type of material at issue in most indecency cases poses no danger for children. They concluded that the sexual nature of double entendre and innuendo is imperceptible to young children, who do not have the moral framework to deal with it. The authors

[24] James Walter Wesolowski, "Obscene, Indecent, or Profane Broadcast Language as Construed by the Federal Courts," Journal of Broadcasting 13:2 (1969): 203-219.

[25] John L. Huffman and Denise M. Trauth, "Obscenity, Indecency, and the Rehnquist Court," Communications and the Law March (1991): 3-23.

[26] Jeremy Harris Lipschultz, "The Influence of the United States Court of Appeals for the District of Columbia Circuit on Broadcast Indecency Policy," Villanova Sports and Entertainment Law Forum 3 (1996): 65.

further concluded that the older children who may understand the innuendo have a developed enough maturity to guard against harm.[27]

Other authors, such as former FCC staff member Edythe Wise, examine the history of indecency as child-centered regulation. Wise traced the evolution of the concept of who society believed should be protected from indecency. She found that the concept of protecting only children from indecency, and not society in general, was a relatively new idea.[28] Another article, published in CommLaw Conspectus, looked at the historical, psychological, and legal perspectives on children and sex in the media. It, too, framed indecency regulation as child-centered regulation.[29]

A final grouping of articles looks at the reactions of various groups to the regulation of indecency. One article by Jeremy Lipschultz looks at the role of the community in indecency fines. The author took two stations that received fines for indecency and looked at the community reaction. Out of this comparison, he drew a number of conclusions about the community participation in the regulation of indecency.

The final three articles to be discussed here look at the reactions of broadcasters to the regulation of indecency. In Roger Sadler's doctoral dissertation, "The Federal Communications Commission and the Regulation of Indecency, The Evolution of the Concept of Chilling Effects," he traces the development of the concept of the chilling effect in communications literature as well as judicial decisions. He then evaluates the chilling effect as related to

---

27 Edward Donnerstein, Barbara Wilson and Daniel Linz, "On the Regulation of Broadcast Indecency to Protect Children," Journal of Broadcasting & Electronic Media 36 (1992): 111-117.

28 Edythe Wise, "A Historical Perspective on the Protection of Children From Broadcast Indecency," Villanova Sports and Entertainment Law Forum 3 (1996): 15-43.

29 Conspectus, "Sex, Violence, Children & the Media: Legal, Historical & Empirical Perspectives," CommLaw Conspectus 5:Summer (1997): 341-358.

indecency and concludes that there is little proof that such an effect exists.[30] In a similar vein, James Hsuing examined the fears of the broadcast industry following the 1978 Supreme Court decision in Pacifica. He concludes that the industry's fears of wide-scale censorship were unwarranted and that the FCC did not use the power it was granted in Pacifica.[31]

An article by Richard Barton also addresses the industry's reaction to Pacifica. But instead of focusing on the 1978 Supreme Court ruling, "The Lingering Legacy of Pacifica: Broadcasters' Freedom of Silence" discusses the 1964 Pacifica actions. Barton focuses on the silence of the industry while Pacifica was being investigated by Congress and the Commission. He concludes that the industry only speaks up in defense of the First Amendment when its financial interests are at stake.

As this portion of the literature review shows, research on indecency is plentiful, but none of the material presented here has made any attempt to look at the history of indecency regulation from the policy-making perspective, nor has any attention been paid to the citizen groups who have been so active in the anti-indecency cause. For that reason, two additional sections are required. The next section examines the literature on citizen groups at the FCC. Finally, this review looks at research that has used the Krasnow, Longley, and Terry model.

Citizen Groups at the FCC

Before the 1960s, the public had little influence at the FCC. Unless a person or group had a financial stake in the matter, he or she had no standing to participate in most FCC proceedings. But that changed when the United Church

---

[30] Roger L. Sadler, "The Federal Communications Commission and the Regulation of Indecency, The Evolution of the Concept of Chilling Effects" (Ph.D. Diss., Indiana University, 1992).

[31] James C. Hsiung, "Indecent Broadcast: An Assessment of Pacifica's Impact," Communications and the Law February (1987): 41-56.

of Christ sought to challenge the renewal of Jackson, Mississippi television station WLBT. The Court of Appeals for the District of Columbia ruled that citizen groups represented the public and therefore the FCC should consult them when considering the public interest.[32] Since then, much has been written on the role of citizen groups at the FCC.

The relationship between citizen groups and the FCC can take many forms, but the research largely concentrates on two types of citizen participation: filing petitions to deny a license renewal and citizen-broadcaster agreements. The petition to deny, filed at a station's license renewal time, informs the FCC that the citizen group, as representatives of the public, believes that the station has not fulfilled its obligation to serve the public interest, convenience, and necessity.[33] The citizen-broadcaster agreements evolved as a reaction to petitions to deny. In the early 1970s, the FCC encouraged the stations to negotiate with the citizen groups that had filed a petition to deny in an effort to improve the stations' public interest performance.[34] The agreements usually resulted in the withdrawal of the petition to deny.[35]

Several articles report the evolution of the use of the petition to deny and agreements by citizen groups. Foremost among this research is a study funded by the Markle Foundation and written by Joseph Grundfest that extensively recounts the rise and fall of the power of the groups at the FCC.[36] The study's documentation of the lack of success in getting licenses revoked is cited in nearly every work on the topic.

---

[32] Office of Communication of the United Church of Christ v. FCC, 359 F.2d 994 (D.C. Cir. 1966).

[33] Krasnow, Longley, and Terry, 54.

[34] Krasnow, Longley, and Terry, 56.

[35] Krasnow, Longley, and Terry, 56.

[36] Joseph A. Grundfest, Citizen Participation in Broadcast Licensing Before the FCC (Santa Monica, CA: The Rand Corporation, with help from a grant from the Markle Foundation, 1976), R-1896-MF.

Another historical review of citizen groups and the FCC is Ronald Garay's "Access: Evolution of the Citizen Agreement."[37] This shorter piece focuses exclusively on the citizen agreement, tracing the FCC's initial acceptance of the concept to its eventual rejection. One reason for that rejection by the Commission was that some citizen groups began to abuse the process. Many petitions to deny were filed merely as a means to extort money and programming control from the stations. The FCC began to consider many of the agreements as an unlawful abdication of control by the stations. The title of a later article, "Tying the Victim's Hands: Curbing Citizen Group Abuse of the Broadcast Licensing Process," is representative of the change in attitude at the FCC about citizen agreements. This article documents the Commission's attempts to block the unsavory groups, who sought nothing except what was in their own, generally monetary, interests rather than the public's interest.[38]

One book, in particular, provides a substantive look at the history of this relationship between the FCC and citizen groups. In Citizens' Groups and Broadcasting,[39] Donald L. Guimary presents a history of citizen groups stretching back to the radio councils of the 1920s. In addition, he presents the stance on citizen groups of the industry, Congress, the courts, the FCC, and even the six commissioners sitting at the time he wrote the book. He then uses three case studies to determine the "paradigm" of what a citizen group should be. Although this comprehensive history, a weakness from the standpoint of current understanding is that it was written in 1975, the zenith of the citizen group movement. The author, who did not foresee the era of deregulation, wrote, "it

---

[37] Ronald Garay, "Access: Evolution of the Citizen Agreement," Journal of Broadcasting 22:1 (1978): 95-106.
[38] Jared L. Burden, "Tying the Victim's Hands: Curbing Citizen Group Abuse of the Broadcast Licensing Process," Federal Communications Law Journal 39:October (1987): 259-295.
[39] Donald L. Guimary, Citizens' Groups and Broadcasting (New York: Praeger Publishers, 1975), 170.

seems likely that the Commission will continue to adapt new policies and regulation to assist public participation."[40]

Research on citizen groups and the FCC often goes beyond merely providing the history of the relationship. Authors have frequently used case studies to reach conclusions about the efficacy of the citizen groups. Some have concluded that the citizens groups have largely failed to affect the FCC in any way. Others accept the apparent quantitative failure but see success in other areas.

Both Jan Linker and James Wollert did quantitative analyses of citizen participation at the FCC. Linker found that not only are groups not successful at the Commission, but they often have a negative effect on commissioner's decisions.[41] Linker describes the groups as "one-shotters," people who are outsiders at the Commission and unfamiliar with its procedures. She writes that while a minority of the Commission may be swayed by a citizen group, a majority never is.[42] Similarly, Wollert found that between 1966 and 1975, all but five of the seventeen commissioners seated supported broadcasters over citizen groups more than 87 percent of the time.[43]

Other authors writing on the topic of citizen groups at the Commission acknowledge that the numbers do not show much success. However, many authors find that success can be measured differently. For example, Joel and Muriel Cantor concluded that while the success rate was exceeding low, the

---

[40] Donald L. Guimary, Citizens' Groups and Broadcasting (New York: Praeger Publishers, 1975),151.

[41] Jan Helene Linker, "Public Intervenors and the Public Airwaves: The Effect of Interest Groups on Federal Communications Commission Decisions" (Ph.D. Diss., Emory University, 1981) and Jan Helene Linker, "Public Intervenors and the Public Airwaves: The Effect of Interest Groups on Federal Communications Commission Decisions," in Communications Policy and the Political Process, ed. J. J. Havick (Westport, CT: Greenwood Press, 1983), 223.

[42] Linker, Public Intervenors (1981), 116.

[43] James Alvin Wollert, "Regulatory Decision-Making: The Federal Communications Commission (1966-1975)" (Ph.D. Diss., Michigan State University, 1976).

decision to allow citizen groups access to the licensing process was an enormous empowerment for these groups.[44] In a similar vein, Cherie Lewis found that while women's groups did not succeed in getting a license revoked, they achieved legitimation, leverage, and publicity.[45] In addition, the petitions to deny and the negotiation of citizen agreements often sensitized broadcasters to the problems of women.

These conclusions about the successes of citizen groups in sensitizing the industry and the Commission were confirmed in a panel discussion held on the tenth anniversary of the United Church of Christ decision. At that time, an FCC attorney stated that while citizen group participation appears to be a dismal failure on the surface, the groups were highly successful in sensitizing the Commission to problems and making it more responsive to the public.[46]

In a study of educational broadcasting and political interest groups, Paul Nord found another way in which groups can succeed at the FCC. In a long term study, Nord discovered that the interest groups who were lobbying for a set-aside of frequencies for educational broadcast stations were pivotal in bringing it into existence. He concludes that the groups were key in setting the parameters of the debate, and thus, their views eventually prevailed.[47]

Despite the focus on the petition to deny and citizen broadcaster agreements, there are other methods for the public to participate in FCC decision-

---

[44] Muriel Cantor and Joel Cantor, "United States: A System of Minimal Regulation," in The Politics of Broadcasting, ed. R. Kuhn (New York: St. Martin's Press, 1985), 158-196.
[45] Cherie Sue Lewis, "Television License Renewal Challenges by Women's Groups" (Ph.D. Diss., University of Minnesota, 1986). Other work reached similar conclusions about symbolic successes of women's groups, see Sarah Slavin and M. Stephen Pendleton, "Feminism and the FCC," in Communications Policy and the Political Process, ed. J. J. Havick (Westport, CT: Greenwood Press, 1983), 223.
[46] Communications Media Center, "When Citizens Complain: *UCC v. FCC* A Decade Later." A panel discussion sponsored by Mass Communications Law Section Association of American Law Schools, New York, 1977.
[47] David Paul Nord, "The FCC, Educational Broadcasting, and Political Interest Group Activity," Journal of Broadcasting 22:3 (1978): 321-338.

making. In "Citizens Groups in Broadcast Regulatory Policy-Making," Longley, Terry, and Krasnow summarize some of the other methods of access, but conclude that deregulation hurt the entry of interest groups into the process.[48] Communication policy scholar Haeryon Kim reached similar conclusions about deregulation. In "The Politics of Deregulation: Public Participation in the FCC Rulemaking Process for DBS,"[49] she goes further to say that in highly technical areas like DBS, the public is at a severe disadvantage. She also concludes that limited time, money and information are significant reasons why the public cannot participate fully in FCC decision-making.

In another look at different ways the public participates in FCC decisions, Michael McGregor examined the efficacy of informal comments filed in rulemaking proceedings.[50] Using three case studies, he found that every comment was read by the staff. Form letters and preprinted postcards were virtually ignored, but a comment from the public that had something novel to offer was taken into serious consideration. He demonstrates that a thoughtful suggestion from a member of the public did appear in the report of the Commission.[51]

The research about citizen groups and the FCC is largely focused on a few methods of entry and mostly demonstrate that symbolic victories are the only victories to be won. This bears out the weak influence of citizen groups that Krasnow, Longley, and Terry present in the broadcast policy-making model. But

---

[48] Lawrence D Longley, Herbert A. Terry, and Erwin G. Krasnow. "Citizens Groups in Broadcast Regulatory Policy-Making." Policy Studies Journal 12 (2): (1983): 258-270.

[49] Haeryon Kim, "The Politics of Deregulation: Public Participation in the FCC Rulemaking Process for DBS," Telecommunications Policy 19:1 (1995): 51-60.

[50] For a submission to be considered a formal comment, it has to follow certain formatting requirements. In addition, anyone filling a formal comment must submit multiple copies. McGregor focuses on those letters that were submitted by the public that did not follow the formatting and multiple copy guidelines.

[51] Michael A. McGregor, "The FCC's Use of Informal Comments in Rule-Making Proceedings," Journal of Broadcasting and Electronic Media 30:4 (1986): 413-425.

the literature fails to address the more general question of why the citizen groups fail.

Krasnow, Longley, and Terry

The final body of literature presented here is the work that tests the Krasnow, Longley, and Terry model of the broadcast policy-making system. This literature has largely used the case-study method. Authors have taken a variety of issues, both controversial and non-controversial and tested the Krasnow, Longley, and Terry model. Of the research presented here, three authors find the model flawed but still useful and three authors believe it is too flawed to be of any use.

In a study of the issue of television violence and Congress, Cynthia Cooper examined the role of Congressional hearings through the lens of the Krasnow, Longley, and Terry model.[52] She concluded that the model is good structurally. But she also concluded that the interaction between Congress and the citizen groups concerned with violence was "most significant." This is in contrast to the Krasnow, Longley, and Terry determination that the relationship between Congress and citizen groups was "less significant."

In two other studies using the model, the authors concluded that although it was basically sound, it was still flawed. Both David E. Tucker and Jeffrey Saffelle's "The Federal Communications Commission and the Regulation of Children's Television"[53] and Peter Seel's "High-Definition Television and United States Telecommunication Policy"[54] found that the model lacked any provision for miscellaneous actors who may have an impact on the policy-making process.

---

[52] Cynthia A. Cooper, "The Role of Congressional Hearings in the Formation of Policy Toward Violence on Television: An Analysis Using the Broadcast Policy-Making System" (Ph.D. Diss., University of Tennessee, 1995).

[53] David E. Tucker and Jeffrey Saffelle, "The Federal Communications Commission and the Regulation of Children's Television," Journal of Broadcasting 26:3 (1982): 657-669.

In Tucker and Saffelle's look at children's television, the authors found that the Federal Trade Commission and the corporate sponsors of children's television were major players in the regulation. But there is no place for them in the model. Similarly, in Seel's look at HDTV, the author found the lack of a role for the Federal Trade Commission a problem. Another matter on which the two studies agreed was that the model lacked accommodation for the environment surrounding the regulatory actors. They assert that Krasnow, Longley, and Terry make no provision for taking things like public opinion and political culture into consideration.

Seel went further with criticism that Tucker and Saffelle did not present. In his study of the dynamics of HDTV, he found that the model fails to explain the process of influence. He believes that just identifying the channels of influence is not enough. In addition, Seel writes that the model does not work well with international issues like HDTV. Despite this criticism, Seel does believe in the underlying strength of the model. Three other authors, however, disagree.

In "FCC Policy on Minority Ownership in Broadcasting: A Political Systems Analysis of Regulatory Policymaking," Marilyn Fife uses the Krasnow, Longley, and Terry model to look at minority ownership.[55] Fife concludes, like Tucker, Saffelle, and Seel, that the environment is missing from the model. Unlike the other researchers, Fife sees this as a fatal flaw. She writes that because the public attitude on race played such a major role in the decision-making process of the FCC, to ignore it compromises the efficacy of the model.

In his doctoral dissertation, Ralph Carmode also chose to use the Krasnow, Longley, and Terry model to analyze FCC policy-making. Carmode

---

[54] Peter Benjamin Seel, "High-Definition Television and United States Telecommunication Policy" (Ph.D. Diss., Indiana University, 1995).

[55] Marilyn Diane Fife, "FCC Policy on Minority Ownership in Broadcasting: A Political Systems Analysis of Regulatory Policymaking" (Ph.D. Diss., Stanford University, 1983).

attempted to test the model by considering a less controversial, less monetarily significant case study: educational FM radio.[56] The study finds many of the same flaws raised by other authors. He found that the environment was not adequately taken into consideration. He also found that miscellaneous actors, this time the Corporation for Public Broadcasting, were not accounted for. In addition, Carmode found that the model lacked a role for the mass media, something he saw as important. Finally, not all of the six regulatory actors outline by Krasnow, Longley, and Terry participated in this action. He felt that this possibility was not explained well by the model.

Haeryon Kim is one of Krasnow, Longley, and Terry's biggest critics.[57] Many of her articles, particularly those that study the policy history of Direct Broadcast Satellite and deregulation, focus on flaws in the model beyond those that have already been discussed. Among other things, Kim writes that the deregulation of the communications industry is such a total paradigm shift that the model is no longer valid. In addition, the FCC's actions on DBS represent a major shift in policy because DBS was a radical change, not incremental as theorized by Krasnow, Longley, and Terry. Finally, she also concludes that the explosion of new technologies has so fractured the "industry" as to make the industry as a policy actor a meaningless term.

A final article did not use the case study method to analyze the Krasnow, Longley, and Terry model. Instead, Elizabeth Mahan and Jorge Reina Schement performed a meta-analysis of broadcast regulatory studies and concluded, like

---

[56] Ralph Edward Carmode, "An Analysis of the Broadcast Policy-Making System an its Application to Federal Communications Commission Docket 20735" (Ph.D. Diss., Pennsylvania State University, 1986).

[57] Haeryon Kim, "Theorizing Deregulation: An Exploration of the Utility of the 'Broadcast Policy-Making System' Model," Journal of Broadcasting & Electronic Media 36:2 (1992): 153-173; Haeryon Kim, "Congressional Influence on the FCC: An Analysis of Confirmation hearings for Commission Chairmen, 1969-1989," Communications and the Law 15:4 (1993): 37-54; and

many of the works mentioned above, that the model does not adequately take the environment surrounding the regulatory actors into consideration.[58]

Summary of the Literature

The literature presented above represents the span of research in three areas: indecency, citizen groups at the FCC, and the usefulness of the Krasnow, Longley and Terry model of the broadcast policy-making system. While the previous sections presented the individual research, this section looks at the sum of the knowledge in each of these three fields.

Much research has been done on the topic of indecency and the attempts to regulate it. Many authors present descriptive, in-depth looks at the facts of what has happened. There is little in the factual history of indecency regulation that has not been written about. In addition, research has been done that presents the facts of what material has been found indecent by the Federal Communications Commission. This research found that there are no definitive guidelines as to what material might be considered indecent by the Commission. Research also shows that most scholars consider the regulation of indecency unconstitutional. While the authors use a variety methods to reach this conclusion, they rarely explain why the courts have consistently ruled that the regulation is, in fact, constitutional. Thus, a review of the literature of indecency demonstrates that while the question of "what has happened?" is successfully answered by the literature, the answer to the question of "why it has happened?" remains unclear.

Haeryon Kim, "The Politics of Deregulation: Public Participation in the FCC Rulemaking Process for DBS," Telecommunications Policy 19:1 (1995): 51-60.

[58] Elizabeth Mahan and Jorge Reina Schement, "The Broadcast Regulatory Process: Toward a New Analytical Framework," in Progress in Communication Sciences, ed. B. Dervin and M. J. Voigt (Norwood, NJ: ABLEX Publishing Corporation, 1984), 1-22.

The issue of the harms that can result from exposure of minors to indecent material is also vastly under-explored territory. While social science literature is filled with empirical research on the effects of violence and pornography, no scientific studies have been done on the effects of exposure to indecent language.[59] Thus, while indecency regulation is based on the need to protect children, no such harm has ever been proven to exist.

Past research into the activities of citizen groups at the Federal Communications Commission is also fairly narrow in its focus. Much of the literature does not look beyond petitions to deny and the citizens-broadcasters agreements that developed in the 1970s. Like the research on indecency, much of the citizen group literature focuses on the history of the groups at the FCC. Research that provided some additional measure of analysis found that the movement was damaged by deregulation and abuse of the process. Most research into this topic, however, has ignored many of the ways that a citizen group might influence the process besides the petition to deny. In addition, the literature has also largely failed to investigate why the groups have had little success at the Commission.

A review of the research that has utilized or critiqued the Krasnow, Longley, and Terry model is fairly evenly split between supporters and detractors. Some researchers have found it hopelessly flawed. Others have concluded that the model, while not perfect, is a good representation of the policy process. The only conclusion that can be extracted from the review of the literature is that the model is important enough to be discussed.

The present research fills some gaps in this literature. By examining the policy process that led to the regulation of indecency, rather than the history of that regulation, this research seeks answers to the "why" question. While it is known what has happened in the history of the regulation, determining the level of impact of citizen groups at the Commission can begin to uncover why the Commission did what it did. In addition, no other research has documented the history of the activities of anti-indecency citizen groups.

The present research is also unique in the wide range of citizen group activity that it describes. The literature on citizen groups is largely limited to the petition to deny and citizen-broadcaster agreement. This research looks beyond that to consider the complaint process, the formal comment process, lobbying, and testimony at Congressional hearings. This wider view of group activity paints a more accurate picture of reality and thus furthers the understanding of the role of citizen groups at the Commission.

---

[59] Donnerstein, 111.

Chapter 3
The History Of Indecency Regulation

While the focus of this research is on the politics behind the regulation of indecency, the history of this regulation must also be presented. In order to discuss the role played by the American Family Association and Morality in Media, it is necessary to understand the context and the times in which they were operating. In addition, the history of the regulation serves to highlight periods of change, times when the groups perhaps had the best opportunity to affect the policies of the FCC. This chapter covers the regulation of indecency from 1962 to the resignation of FCC Chairman Reed Hundt at the end of 1997.

The history of the regulation of broadcast indecency by the FCC is complex. The Radio Act of 1927 included a section[1] that banned the use of "obscene, indecent or profane language" over the radio airwaves.[2] This restriction was carried through all of the changes in communications law over the last sixty years, but only occasionally enforced for much of that time. There is no definitive beginning to the policy, and scholarly opinion on this topic varies widely. While the presence of section 1464 demonstrates that there have been concerns about

---

[1] 18 U.S.C. 1464

[2] 44 Stat. 1172 (1927).

sexual material on the broadcast airwaves since the beginning of broadcasting itself,[3] this research begins with the 1962 Palmetto decision.

Early Attempts at Regulation

The early attempts to regulate indecency on broadcasting were an effort by the FCC to make some sense of the statutory ban on obscene, indecent, and profane language. Through these years, the Commission struggled over how to define indecent language as separate from obscenity. While the constitutionality of the definition of obscenity had been ruled on by the Supreme Court many times, the term "indecent" had not undergone the same judicial scrutiny. It was then up to the Commission to make the determination of what material would be considered indecent, and thus unacceptable on the broadcast airwaves.

An early attempt to address the question of the definition of indecency came when the FCC decided not to renew the license of WDKD, Kingstree, South Carolina. In a case officially called In re Palmetto Broadcasting Company,[4] but more commonly known as the Charlie Walker case,[5] the FCC reluctantly began the struggle to define what would and would not be considered indecent.[6]

Walker was a popular WDKD personality known for his off-color humor and sexually-suggestive jokes.[7] In 1959, an employee from a neighboring station recorded "The Charlie Walker Show" and sent the tapes to the FCC.[8] The Commission contacted Edward Robinson, WDKD's owner, regarding the

---

[3]Milagros Rivera-Sanchez, "Developing an Indecency Standard: The Federal Communications Commission and the Regulation of Offensive Speech, 1927-1964," Journalism History 20:1 (1994): 3-14.

[4] 33 FCC 250 (1961).

[5] For a detailed history of this case, see F. Leslie Smith, "The Charlie Walker Case," Journal of Broadcasting 23:2 (1979): 137-151.

[6] Henry Geller, FCC general counsel and author of the *Palmetto* decision said in an interview quoted in Rivera-Sanchez, "Developing an Indecency Standard," 9 that the FCC was not anxious to tread on this constitutionally-charged ground.

[7] Smith, 137.

program. He denied having any knowledge of the suggestive nature of the programs and told the FCC that he fired Walker once he had learned of the show's content.[9] Despite these moves, the FCC scheduled a renewal hearing to determine, among other things, whether Robinson was exercising proper control over the programming and whether the Walker broadcasts were indecent.[10]

At the hearing, a number of people testified that Robinson did, in fact, know the content of the Walker show.[11] As a result, the hearing examiner concluded that Robinson had misrepresented facts to the Commission and had failed to maintain adequate control over the programming.[12] In addition, the examiner concluded that Walker had broadcast "coarse, vulgar and suggestive material susceptible of indecent double meaning."[13] The Commission, wary of the constitutional issues, based the denial of renewal on the less-controversial grounds of misrepresentation.[14]

Robinson challenged the non-renewal of his license to the U.S. Court of Appeals for the District of Columbia.[15] The FCC based its case on the misrepresentation, but also asked the court to rule on the issue of whether a pattern of broadcasts that contained coarse, vulgar and suggestive material susceptible of indecent double meaning was a violation of the public interest.[16] Robinson, with the support of the ACLU, based his challenge on First

---

[8] 33 FCC 265, 276-277.
[9] 33 FCC 265, 267.
[10] 33 FCC 265, 265.
[11] 33 FCC 265, 274-276.
[12] 33 FCC 265, 266-267.
[13] 33 FCC 265, 276
[14] 33 FCC 250 (1962). For a look at the political concerns of the Commission, see Rivera-Sanchez, Regulatory History, 110.
[15] Robinson v. FCC, 334 F.2d 534 (1964).
[16] Robinson v. FCC, U.S. Court of Appeals for the District of Columbia, Brief for Appellant, Case No. 17, 587, FCC Library, Brief No. 251C, 5 July 1963, 3, as cited in Rivera-Sanchez, Regulatory History, 113.

Amendment grounds.[17] The court sidestepped the constitutional issue by ruling solely that the FCC had the right to not renew a license on the grounds that a licensee had lied to the Commission.[18] Although one judge on the panel discussed the topic of content regulation in a concurrence, the parameters of what would be considered indecent speech went unreviewed.

In January, 1964, the Commission released a Memorandum Opinion and Order renewing the licenses of Pacifica Foundation stations KPFA-FM, KPFB-FM, and WBAI-FM, as well as granting a license for KPFK-FM.[19] Because of some complaints and a Congressional inquiry involving accusations of communism,[20] the Commission issued the Order to address the controversy. The FCC considered three areas: programming, Communist Party affiliation, and a question of unauthorized transfer of control of the station. The Communist issues, as well as the unauthorized transfer were readily dismissed in a few paragraphs; the main focus of the Order was the controversial programming.

The content of five programs broadcast between 1959 and 1963 were examined in order to determine if they met the public interest responsibilities of the licensee or represented a pattern of offensive broadcasting, like in Palmetto.[21] Three of the broadcasts were found to be squarely within the scope of the station's public interest responsibilities: Edward Albee's acclaimed play The Zoo Story; "Live and Let Live," a panel discussion concerning homosexuality; and a reading from Edward Pomerantz's unfinished novel, The Kid.[22] The Commission concluded that while the programs might be offensive to some, its licensing power

---

[17] Rivera-Sanchez, Regulatory History, 116.
[18] 334 F.2d 534.
[19] 1 Rad. Reg.2d (P& F) 747 (1964).
[20] Hearings Before the Subcommittee to Investigate the Administration of the Internal Security Act and Other Internal Security Laws of the Committee of the Judiciary, United States Senate, 88th Cong., 1st Sess. (1963). See also Richard L. Barton, "The Lingering Legacy of Pacifica: Broadcasters' Freedom of Silence," Journalism Quarterly 53:3 (1976): 429-433.
[21] 1 Rad. Reg.2d (P& F) 749.

did not allow it to rule controversial programming from the airwaves.[23] Pacifica admitted that the other two programs in question, poetry readings from Lawrence Ferlinghetti and Robert Creeley, should not have been broadcast. But Pacifica offered explanations that satisfied the Commission.[24] The FCC concluded that two errors, separated by four years, did not represent a pattern of offensive broadcasting like the one found in Palmetto and the licenses were renewed.[25]

In 1965, however, the fate of the Pacifica stations KPFA-FM, KPFB-FM, and KPFK-FM was again in question. In December of that year, the Commission issued short-term renewals for these licenses.[26] Again, controversial programming was at issue. This time Pacifica said that some broadcasts had deviated from the Foundation's standards because of some personnel changes. Pacifica claimed that the situation had been rectified and the offending broadcasts would not happen again. The FCC acknowledged that the changes seemed to be working, but nonetheless ordered the short-term renewals. Commissioners Cox and Loevinger, as well as Chairman Henry, dissented from the decision, calling the KPFK incident "isolated."[27] In addition, they pointed out that the WBAI license was not even up for renewal for another six months. The dissenters recommended that the licenses be renewed for a full term.

In 1969, Pacifica stations KPFA-FM, KPFB-FM, and KPFK-FM were again in the spotlight. In a Memorandum Opinion and Order released by the Commission in February, the licenses were renewed after addressing complaints

---

[22] 1 Rad. Reg.2d (P& F) 749, 750.
[23] 1 Rad. Reg.2d (P& F) 749, 750.
[24] Pacifica claimed that it broadcast the Ferlinghetti tape with minimal screening because of his national reputation. Pacifica admitted that the decision to do so was wrong. In addition, Pacifica argued that the Creeley tape was read in a monotonous voice, with eighteen acceptable poems preceding the offensive one and nine after. Again, Pacifica admitted that the broadcast was a mistake. 1 Rad. Reg.2d 749, 751.
[25] 1 Rad. Reg.2d 749, 751.
[26] 6 Rad. Reg.2d 570 (1965).
[27] 6 Rad. Reg.2d 570, 571.

about controversial programming.[28] Without detailing any of the specific broadcasts in question, the FCC merely stated that complainants found the programming "a one-sided view of this 'new left' movement, advocating open warfare on the streets" and "disgusting and totally without redeeming qualities."[29] Despite these complaints, the Commission chose to reiterate its January 1964 Pacifica opinion that stated it could not ban provocative programming.[30]

The last major incident in the history of indecency before the issuance of the first fine came in the case of a station licensed to the Jack Straw Memorial Foundation. KRAB-FM, a small, listener-supported station in Seattle was given a one year renewal for violating its own policy against "obscenity, obscurantism, sensationalism, or simple boorishness."[31] According to the FCC, "the critical consideration is not whether or not action under 18 U.S.C. 1464 is warranted. . . . [It is] whether KRAB-FM is exercising proper supervision of its operations and specifically is following its stated policies in this area."[32]

The station planned to broadcast a thirty-hour autobiography from a local pastor named Reverend Paul Sawyer. The president of the station, Lorenzo Milam, auditioned portions of the tape and cleared it for broadcast after determining that the content and presentation were interesting. The broadcast began on a Saturday morning and Milam was at home listening. At some point, he heard language that he found inappropriate and called the station. Reverend Sawyer, who was at the station monitoring the program, assured Milam that the language would not reoccur. Sometime later in the broadcast, Milam heard the

---

[28] 16 FCC.2d 712 (1969).
[29] 16 FCC.2d 712, 713.
[30] 16 FCC.2d 712, 713.
[31] 21 FCC.2d 833 (1970).
[32] 21 FCC.2d 833.

language again and called the station a second time. He then drove to the station and took the program off the air. The FCC received one complaint.[33]

The Commission considered no tape or transcript of the program in its determination of the short-term renewal. In fact, according to Commissioner Kenneth A. Cox's dissent, the FCC did not even know in what context the words, which were not listed in the FCC documents, were broadcast. The station asked for a reconsideration, but the FCC denied the petition.[34] KRAB then requested that an evidentiary hearing be held. The Commission granted that request, but only if the hearing focused on more than simply the broadcast at issue.[35] Eventually, the Commission granted a full renewal. In fact, the hearing examiner concluded that "KRAB's programming is meritorious and the station does render an outstanding broadcast service to the area which it serves."[36] The station was, thus, awarded a full-term renewal.

While the order announcing the short-term renewal of KRAB-FM specifically stated that section 1464 was not the issue, the action does appear to fit a pattern of increased attention to the broadcast of offensive material that was brewing at the Commission.[37] The next section details the more concentrated attempts at regulation, including the early fines and the George Carlin broadcast.

Defining the Parameters

Beginning in 1970, the FCC attempted to face the problem of broadcast indecency head-on. Concerned about the constitutional issues at stake, the Commission sought a test case to provide it with a judicial review of the

[33] Interestingly, the facts of this case are only sketchily presented in the majority opinion. This information is from the dissent of Commissioner Kenneth Cox, who was scathing in his criticism of the decision.
[34] 24 FCC.2d 266 (1970).
[35] 26 FCC.2d 97 (1970).
[36] 29 FCC.2d 334 (1971).

parameters of indecency as a separate concept from obscenity.[38] In the first few years of the decade, the FCC handed down two fines for the broadcast of indecent material in the hopes a station would appeal.

The first station fined was WUHY-FM, a non-commercial educational radio station in Pennsylvania licensed to Eastern Education Radio. WUHY garnered the indecency charge by broadcasting a taped interview with Grateful Dead front man Jerry Garcia on a regularly scheduled program called "CYCLE II," airing from 10:00 to 11:00 p.m. Throughout the interview, Garcia used "two of the most celebrated Anglo-Saxon four letter words . . . with remarkable frequency."[39] The FCC deemed this material indecent, concluding that "the speech involved has no redeeming social value, and is patently offensive by contemporary community standards, with very serious consequences to the public interest in the larger and more effective use of radio."[40] The Commission issued an $100 fine. It invited WUHY to seek judicial review to further clarify the indecency ruling.[41] WUHY, unwilling to pursue a lengthy and expensive law suit, paid the fine.[42]

---

[37] See Rivera-Sanchez, Regulatory History, 152.
[38] In Re WUHY-FM, 24 F.C.C.2d 408 (1970), the FCC wrote, "On this issue, we note that, in view of the fact that this is largely a case of first impression, particularly as to the Section 1464 aspect, we could appropriately forego the forfeiture and simply act prospectively in this field. . . . However, were we to do so, we would prevent any review of our action and in this sensitive field we have always sought to insure such reviewability. . . We believe that a most crucial peg underlying all Commission action in the programming field is the vital consideration that the courts are there to review and reverse any action which runs afoul of the First Amendment. Thus, while we think that our action is fully consistent with the law, there should clearly be the avenue of court review in a case of this nature (see Section 504 (a)). Indeed, we would welcome such review, since only in that way can the pertinent standards be definitively determined." The FCC expressed similar sentiments in the Sonderling case, 41 F.C.C.2d 777 (1973).
[39] 24 FCC.2d 408. The words were shit and fuck.
[40] 24 FCC.2d 408, 409.
[41] 24 FCC.2d 408, 410.
[42] Don M. Gillmor, Jerome A. Barron, T. F. Simon and Herbert A. Terry, "The Regulation of Electronic Media," in Mass Communications Law: Cases and Comment, (St. Paul: West Publishing Company, 1990), 825-828., 827.

WUHY-FM was a small station broadcasting to the counter-culture youth of the early seventies. The next target of the FCC, however, was the popular "Topless Radio."[43]

Begun in 1971 at a Los Angeles radio station, topless radio consisted of women phoning in to discuss intimate sexual matters with a male host. The format soon spread to nearly every major market in the country.[44] The FCC, particularly Chairman Dean Burch, took notice. In a scathing speech before the National Association of Broadcasters on March 28, 1973, Burch warned broadcasters that this type of "smut" would not be tolerated.[45]

Shortly thereafter, on April 11, the FCC notified Sonderling Broadcasting of a $2,000 fine for indecent and obscene programming.[46] The licensee in question, WGLD in Oak Park, Illinois, had been broadcasting a program called "Femme Forum," a typical "topless radio" show. The FCC once again encouraged the licensee to seek judicial review, stating "we welcome and urge judicial consideration of our action."[47] Like WUHY, Sonderling chose to pay the forfeiture. In addition, it canceled "Femme Forum." Most of the other stations around the country followed suit and Topless Radio disappeared from the radio scene.[48]

While Sonderling refused to pursue judicial review, a group called the Illinois Citizens Committee for Broadcasting, along with the Illinois ACLU, challenged the FCC's action. ICCB requested that, among other things, the FCC remit the Sonderling fine.[49] The Commission refused and the case went to the

---

[43] John C. Carlin, "The Rise and Fall of Topless Radio," Journal of Communication Winter (1976): 31-37.
[44] Carlin, 32.
[45] Carlin, 31.
[46] 41 FCC.2d 919 (1973).
[47] 41 FCC.2d 919, 921.
[48] Carlin, 36.
[49] 41 FCC.2d 777 (1973).

U.S. Circuit Court of Appeals for the District of Columbia. In Illinois Citizens Committee for Broadcasting v. FCC,[50] the court upheld the Commission's findings. The court held that the Commission had proven that Sonderling's broadcasts were obscene.[51] The question of the lesser standard for indecency was dismissed by the courts, which said that if the licensee had refused to pay the fine and demanded a jury trial, the question of indecency could have been addressed.[52]

While Eastern Education Radio and Sonderling both refused to pursue judicial review of the FCC's attempts at regulating indecent speech, the Pacifica Foundation was not so reluctant. An incident involving Pacifica station WBAI-FM sparked the complaint that eventually led all the way to the U.S. Supreme Court.

In the early afternoon of October 30, 1973, John R. Douglas, a minister from Florida and a member of the National Planning Board of Morality in Media, claimed to be driving around New York City with his fifteen-year-old son and tuned his radio into WBAI.[53] The program he heard was a regularly scheduled, live discussion called "Lunchpail," hosted by Paul Gorman. That afternoon's program involved an analysis of contemporary attitudes towards language and included a segment of comedian George Carlin's Occupation: Foole album. The twelve-minute monologue, called "Filthy Words," was preceded by a warning and featured a lengthy recitation of various forms of "the words you couldn't say on the public airways."[54] Mr. Douglas heard only the monologue and took great offense to this broadcast of "garbage," and complained to the FCC.[55] The

---

[50] 515 F.2d 397 (1974).
[51] 515 F.2d 397, 405.
[52] 515 F.2d 397, 405.
[53] Lois P. Sheinfeld, "FCC Doublespeak," Film Comment, September/October, 87-90.
[54] George Carlin, Occupation: Foole, Little David Records. The seven filthy words are shit, piss, fuck, cunt, cocksucker, motherfucker and tits.
[55] In the Matter of a Citizen's Complaint Against Pacifica Foundation Station WBAI, 56 FCC.2d 94 (1975).

Commission forwarded the complaint to Pacifica for comment, but took no further action at that time.

Then, in 1974, Congress directed the FCC to prepare a report on "specific positive action taken and planned by the Commission to protect children from excessive programming of violence and obscenity."[56] On February 12, 1975, just one week prior to submitting the "Report on the Broadcast of Violent, Indecent and Obscene Material," the FCC adopted a Declaratory Order citing the "Lunchpail" broadcast as actionably indecent.[57] Indecency was now defined as material that "describes in terms patently offensive to contemporary community standards for the broadcast medium, sexual or excretory activities or organs, at times of the day when there is a reasonable risk that children may be in the audience."[58]

In addition to providing an explicit definition of indecency, the FCC also established the concept of a safe harbor. The Commission asserted that explicit material is actionable only if there is a "reasonable risk" that children may be in the audience. But, if the material is broadcast at a time when the presence of children under the age of twelve is at a minimum, "a different standard might conceivably be used."[59]

Although no fine was issued, a letter was placed in WBAI's file for consideration at license renewal time.[60] That letter was also included in the Appendix of the report to Congress.[61] With support from the ACLU, Pacifica

[56]See H.R. Rep. No. 1139, 93d Cong., 2nd Sess. (1974), 15; and S. Rep. No. 1056, 93d Cong., 2nd Sess. (1974).
[57] 56 FCC.2d 94 (1975).
[58] 56 FCC.2d 94.
[59] 56 FCC.2d 94, 98.
[60] 56 FCC.2d 94, 99.
[61] Report on the Broadcast of Violent, Indecent, and Obscene Material, 32 Rad. Reg.2d 1367 (1973).

agreed to seek judicial review and filed an appeal with the U.S. Court of Appeals for the District of Columbia.

Before the Pacifica case reached oral arguments, the FCC took action against another station. WXPN-FM was a student-run station licensed to the University of Pennsylvania. The Commission found that in December of 1975, a program called "The Vegetable Report" violated the laws against obscenity and indecency.[62] Despite the fact that the University subsequently took greater control over the station and suspended the personnel responsible, the FCC issued a fine of $2,000 for the broadcast of obscene and indecent material.[63] A few weeks later, the station's license renewal application was designated for a hearing.[64] An administrative law judge determined that the University had not maintained adequate control of the programming[65] and the Commission denied renewal.[66]

Not long after "The Vegetable Report" incident, the FCC and the Pacifica Foundation faced off in the D.C. Circuit.[67] Pacifica challenged the FCC's definition of indecency on the grounds that the monologue did not appeal to the prurient interest and therefore was not obscene under Miller.[68] In addition, Pacifica argued that the Order was overbroad because it did not provide a protection for programs with serious literary, artistic, political, or scientific value.[69] The FCC argued that restricting indecent speech on the public airwaves was necessary to protect children.[70] The U.S. Court of Appeals for the District

---

[62] 57 FCC.2d 782 (1975).
[63] 57 FCC.2d 782, 789.
[64] 57 FCC.2d 793 (1976).
[65] 70 FCC.2d 1017 (1977).
[66] 69 FCC.2d 1394 (1978), petition for reconsideration denied, 71 FCC.2d 416 (1979).
[67] Pacifica Foundation v. FCC, 556 F.2d 9 (1977).
[68] 556 F.2d 9, 12.
[69] 556 F.2d 9, 13.
[70] 556 F.2d 9, 13.

of Columbia ruled that the definition was unconstitutionally overbroad.[71] The FCC appealed and the Supreme Court of the United States granted certiorari.

The Supreme Court Decision and the Aftermath

In April, 1978, the FCC and the Pacifica Foundation made their oral arguments to the Supreme Court. Once again, Pacifica argued that Carlin's monologue did not appeal to the prurient interest and was therefore not obscene.[72] The Commission continued to argue that the protection of children justified the restriction on speech.[73] In a plurality opinion, the Court found that the Carlin monologue was indecent only "as broadcast."[74] The monologue was fully protected by the First Amendment everywhere but on the public airwaves at times of the day when children might be in the audience. Justice John Paul Stevens wrote that the technology of broadcasting was the key factor in determining whether indecent material can be regulated.[75] Justice Stevens found that broadcasting has a "uniquely pervasive presence," which invades the home uninvited and unexpectedly.[76] An unwilling adult listener could easily stumble upon indecent material without warning in his own home, where he has a greater right to be free of such material.[77] The second aspect of the technology that Justice Stevens claimed made broadcasting different was that it is "uniquely accessible to children, even those too young to read."[78]

---

[71] 556 F.2d 9, 10.
[72] 438 U.S. 726, 740 (1978).
[73] 438 U.S. 726, 739.
[74] 438 U.S. 726, 734.
[75] 438 U.S. 726, 748.
[76] 438 U.S. 726, 748.
[77] 438 U.S. 726, 748-9.
[78] 438 U.S. 726, 748-9.

Many feared that the Supreme Court's decision in Pacifica gave the FCC *carte blanche* to regulate any explicit speech on the broadcast airwaves.[79] These suspicions, however, proved to be unfounded. In a ruling issued shortly after the Pacifica decision, the FCC's clarified its plan of action regarding indecent speech. In Re Application of WGBH Educational Foundation for Renewal of License for Non Commercial Education Station WGBH-TV,[80] the Commission wrote "we intend strictly to observe the narrowness of the Pacifica holding."[81]

The WGBH decision came about because the Massachusetts branch of Morality in Media had petitioned the FCC to deny the station's license renewal on the basis of the broadcast of indecent material.[82] Citing programs like "Masterpiece Theater" and "Monty Python's Flying Circus," the group claimed that the programming was vulgar and harmful to minors.[83] The Commission stated that the Supreme Court's decision was extremely narrow, and that barring another "verbal shock treatment" equivalent to the Carlin monologue, it would take no action.[84] The Commission renewed WGBH's license.

For nine years following the WGBH decision, the FCC was silent on the topic of indecency. Ronald Reagan was elected president on a platform of limited government and deregulation.[85] His FCC Chair, Mark Fowler, was vocal in his belief that marketplace forces were the most appropriate way to govern

---

[79] James C. Hsiung, "Indecent Broadcast: An Assessment of Pacifica's Impact," Communications and the Law February (1987): 41-42. This article cites number of articles that appeared in trade journals like *Broadcasting* and Publisher's *Weekly* that express the fear that broadcasters had after the ruling in *Pacifica.*
[80] 69 FCC.2d 1250 (1978).
[81] 69 FCC.2d 1250, 1254.
[82] 69 FCC.2d 1250, 1250.
[83] 69 FCC.2d 1250, 1251.
[84] 69 FCC.2d 1250, 1254.
[85] Marc Allen Eisner, "Discovering Patterns in Regulatory History: Continuity, Change and Regulatory Regimes," Journal of Policy History 6 (1994): 164.

broadcasting.[86] At the same time, the country saw the rise of a new type of radio personality, known as the shock jock. This brand of innuendo-laden humor invaded morning shows across the country.[87] Once again, the calls to regulate indecency began.[88] From this pressure came the FCC's reentrance into the regulation of indecency: The 1987 April Trio.[89]

The April 1987 Trio

In April 1987, the FCC released three decisions that significantly expanded the scope of indecency.[90] The FCC decided that the simple prohibition of the seven dirty words before ten p.m. was too narrow a policy.[91] The Commission chose to cite three licensees as examples of what material would now be considered indecent: the Pacifica Foundation, the Regents of the University of California, and Infinity Broadcasting. The Pacifica station, KPFK-FM, had broadcast excerpts from a critically-acclaimed play called Jerker, which included graphic descriptions of homosexual encounters.[92] The program was broadcast after ten p.m. and preceded by a warning. The University of California licensee was the student-run station on the Santa Barbara campus. The station, KCSB, played a punk rock song called "Makin' Bacon" sometime after ten p.m. on a Saturday night.[93] The song had a significant amount of sexual innuendo, but none of the seven dirty words. The Commission also cited Infinity Broadcasting's

---

[86] Mark S. Fowler and Daniel L. Brenner, "A Marketplace Approach to Broadcast Regulation," Texas Law Review 60 (1982): 207.
[87] Julia Reed, "Raunch 'n' Roll Radio is Here to Stay," U.S. News and World Report, 4 May 1987, 52.
[88] Lois P. Sheinfeld, "FCC Doublespeak," Film Comment, September/October, 87-90.
[89] Sheinfeld, 87-90.
[90] In the Matter of Pacifica Foundation, Inc, 2 FCC Rcd 2698 (1987); In the Matter of The Regents of the University of California, 2 FCC Rcd 2703 (1987); and In the Matter of Infinity Broadcasting, 2 FCC Rcd 2705 (1987).
[91] 2 FCC Rcd 2698, 2699.
[92] 2 FCC Rcd 2698, 2698.
[93] 2 FCC Rcd 2703.

Howard Stern. The shock-jock's show aired from six a.m. to ten a.m. every weekday morning and, like KCSB, did not use any of the prohibited words. The program, however, was filled with innuendo and double entendre.[94]

These decisions represented a change in policy because two of the broadcasts took place after ten p.m., within the safe harbor established by Pacifica. The Commission declared that "no such arbitrary time of day," such as ten p.m., would protect indecency.[95] The FCC also revisited the definition of indecency, writing that "innuendo can be . . . rendered explicit by surrounding explicit references" and could and would now be found actionable.[96] This was a change from the strict adherence to the seven words at issue in Pacifica. In essence the indecency policy went from no repetitive use of the seven dirty words before ten p.m., to sexual innuendo and no safe harbor.

The licensees, along with organizations such as the National Association of Broadcasters, the broadcast networks, and Action for Children's Television, immediately filed for reconsideration. Released in December 1987, the Reconsideration Order upheld the broadened definition of indecency, and included in a footnote a possible new safe harbor. The FCC stated "12:00 midnight is our current thinking as to when it is reasonable to expect that it is late enough to ensure that the risk of children in the audience is minimized."[97]

A concurrence by Commissioner Patricia Diaz Dennis raised questions about this change in the safe harbor. She suggested that "not only is this dicta, it is neither decisive nor clear."[98] She said that the FCC had not made it clear what exactly it thought about the safe harbor or why it thought that way. In addition, she pointed out that the Commission had established no body of data of its own

---

94 2 FCC Rcd 2705.
95 2 FCC Rcd 2703, 2704.
96 2 FCC Rcd 2703, 2703.
97 3 FCC Rcd 930 (1987).

that supported one safe harbor over another and had never held any rule making procedure to gather such data. Commissioner Dennis, although agreeing that the broadcasts in question were clearly indecent, stated that a reasoned and unambiguous safe harbor was vital to the constitutionality of the indecency policy.[99]

The April Trio cases reintroduced the indecency issue to the agenda of the FCC. For the ten years that followed, the Commission dealt with two distinct facets of the regulation. The first involved litigation over the parameters of the safe harbor. The second concerned the fines issued to stations for the broadcast of indecent material.

The Battle Over the Safe Harbor

Groups like the National Association of Broadcasters and Action for Children's Television were dissatisfied with the FCC's reconsideration of the April Trio cases and filed an appeal. In June of 1988, the U.S. Court of Appeals for the District of Columbia heard oral arguments in Action for Children's Television v. FCC[100] (ACT I), a suit based on that Reconsideration Order. ACT challenged both the generic definition of indecency as well as the new midnight to six a.m. safe harbor established by the FCC. Before the court could hand down its decision, however, Senator Jesse Helms (R-NC) proposed an amendment to a 1989 appropriations bill that banned indecency completely from the broadcast airwaves.[101] This amendment would, in his words, "simply . . . direct the Federal Communications Commission to enforce the law, period."[102] Helms believed that Section 1464 very clearly prohibited indecency from the airwaves. He stated that

---

[98] 3 FCC Rcd 930, 938.
[99] 3 FCC Rcd 930, 938.
[100] 852 F.2d 1332 (D.C. Cir. 1988).
[101] 100 Pub. L. 459; see also 134 Cong. Rec. S 9971 (1998).

the fact that the FCC had taken it upon itself to contradict Congress by creating a safe harbor for "garbage" was "outrageous."[103] According to Helms, the amendment was absolutely necessary because if the safe harbor were allowed to stand, it would do irreparable damage to the moral fiber of this country, causing it to "crumble."[104] The amendment, as approved by voice vote by the rest of the Appropriations Committee and passed by the Senate, stated that:

> By January 31, 1989 the Federal Communications Commission, shall promulgate regulations in accordance with Section 1464, Title 18, United States Code, to enforce the provisions of such Section on a 24 hour per day basis.[105]

The Helms Amendment was not in the House version of this bill, so its fate rested in the hands of a conference committee charged with reconciling the two bills. Before the conference committee could meet, however, the Court of Appeals handed down its decision in Action for Children's Television v. FCC.

The court upheld the generic definition of indecency on the basis that the Supreme Court had done so in Pacifica. But it concluded that the FCC had not justified the change in the safe harbor, calling the decision "arbitrary and capricious" and "more ritual than real."[106] It remanded the two cases involving broadcasts after ten p.m., Jerker and "Makin' Bacon," back to the FCC for reconsideration and upheld one daytime violation levied against Infinity for the broadcast of the "Howard Stern Show." The court stated that although it could not order the FCC to hold a rule making procedure, it strongly suggested the Commission do so.[107]

---

102 134 Cong. Rec. S 9972 (1988).
103 134 Cong. Rec. S 9972
104 134 Cong. Rec. S 9972
105 134 Cong. Rec. S 9972 , S 9971.
106 852 F.2d 1332, 1341 (D.C. Cir. 1988).
107 852 F.2d 1343.

The ACT I court determined that indecency was constitutionally-protected speech.[108] The court also acknowledged that the government had a legitimate interest in the protection of children from that speech.[109] In addition, the First Amendment rights of adults who wished to hear indecent material, and the broadcasters who wished to air it also had to be weighed in the equation.[110] The court concluded that the only way to serve all the interests was a clearly delineated channeling mechanism, a safe harbor.[111]

Shortly after this decision was announced, the conference committee for the appropriations bill approved the Helms Amendment banning indecent material twenty-four hours a day. President Reagan signed the bill into law and the FCC had little choice but to ignore the court's opinion and enforce the complete ban because Helms had made the Commission's funding contingent on the enforcement of the ban.[112] ACT returned to court to challenge the new ban in early 1991 and the Action for Children's Television v. FCC (ACT II) panel found the twenty-four hour ban clearly unconstitutional and, once again, ordered the FCC to create a safe harbor.[113]

Only months after the decision in ACT II, another senator involved himself in the regulation of indecency. During debate over the Public Telecommunications Act of 1992, which served primarily to fund the Corporation for Public Broadcasting, Senator Robert Byrd called television "packaged corruption for the soul"[114] and proposed an amendment that would require the FCC to prohibit the broadcast of indecent programming:

---

[108] 852 F.2d 1343, 1344.
[109] 852 F.2d 1343, 1343-4.
[110] 852 F.2d 1343, 1344.
[111] 852 F.2d 1343, 1344.
[112] Enforcement of Prohibitions Against Broadcast Obscenity and Indecency, 4 FCC Rcd 457 (1988).
[113] 932 F.2d 1504 (D.C. Cir. 1991).
[114] 138 Cong. Rec. S 7308 (1992).

(1) between 6 a.m. and 10 p.m. on any day by any public radio station or public television station that goes off the air at or before 12 midnight; and

(2) between 6 a.m. and 12 midnight on any day for any radio or television broadcasting station not described in paragraph (1).[115]

The Byrd Amendment was offered with the support of Communications Subcommittee Chairman Daniel Inouye (D-Hawaii) and endorsed in writing by Senator Helms. This amendment was approved in the Senate by voice vote, 93-3, on June 3, 1992, as part of a nearly a dozen changes to the overall bill.[116]

Shortly after President Bush signed the bill with the Byrd Amendment, ACT returned to court. Action for Children's Television v. FCC (ACT III) generated two opinions from the Court of Appeals for the D.C. Circuit. The first decision, which completely dismissed the safe harbors set out by the Byrd Amendment, was vacated in lieu of *en banc* rehearing.[117] The court *en banc* said that a midnight ban would have been acceptable, had Congress not provided the ten p.m. exception to those broadcasters who went off the air before midnight. Because there was no justification for this time discrepancy, the court held that a ban from six a.m. until ten p.m. was sufficient to protect minors.[118]

The result of all this litigation is that a safe harbor for the broadcast of indecent material exists from ten p.m. to six a.m., exactly as it stood in 1987.

---

[115] 138 Cong. Rec. S 7308, S 7304.

[116] R. Sukow, "House Passes 6 a.m.-Midnight Ban," Broadcasting, 10 August 1992, 28.

[117] ACT v. FCC (ACT III), 11 F.3d 170 (D.C. Cir. 1993); ACT v. FCC (ACT III: rehearing *en banc*), No. 93-1092. (D.C. Cir. 1995).

[118] ACT v. FCC (ACT III: rehearing *en banc*), No. 93-1092. (D.C. Cir. 1995).

Fines and Settlement

In April of 1987, the FCC released three decisions that had great impact on the way the Commission was going to regulate indecency. The Commission had decided that it was no longer going to limit itself to regulating only the seven dirty words. Those three decisions, Pacifica, KCSB, and Infinity, marked the beginning of a new era of regulation. Deregulation was over [119] and the era of ever-larger indecency fines had arrived.

More than a year passed before the first fine was issued under the new standard. On June 23, 1988, a fine was levied against Missouri television station KZKC-TV for the broadcast of the movie, Private Lessons.[120] The movie featured a housekeeper's seduction of a fifteen-year-old boy and was broadcast at eight p.m.[121] While the station admitted the broadcast was a mistake and fired the person responsible,[122] the FCC chose to issue a $2,000 fine.[123] Shortly thereafter, in response to the decision in ACT I, the Commission stayed the fine.[124] A year after that, in September of 1989, the FCC released an Order that vacated the proceeding against KZKC.[125] The Order was released in response to the ACT II decision by the U.S. Court of Appeals to stay the twenty four-hour ban proposed by Congress.[126] In addition, the Commission used that Order to announce that the safe harbor would now begin at eight p.m., "until such time as further rulings from the courts permit us to conclude otherwise."[127]

---

[119] Caroline E. Mayer, "FCC Curbs Radio, TV Language; Agency Threatens Stations that are Sexually Explicit," The Washington Post, 17 April 1987, A1.
[120] In the Matter of Kansas City Television, 4 FCC Rcd 7653 (1988).
[121] John Burgess, "FCC Fines Missouri TV Station; Penalty is First Under 'Indecency' Rule," The Washington Post, 24 June 1988, D3.
[122] Burgess, "Missouri TV Station," D3.
[123] 4 FCC Rcd 7653.
[124] 4 FCC Rcd 7653.
[125] 4 FCC Rcd 6706 (1989).
[126] 4 FCC Rcd 6706.
[127] 4 FCC Rcd 6706.

Not long after the decision to set the safe harbor from eight p.m. to six a.m., the Commission handed down a fine to radio station WLLZ, Detroit.[128] WLLZ had played a satirical song called, "Walk with an Erection" by the Swinging Erudites, which garnered them a $2,000 fine.[129] Shortly thereafter, the Commission announced that it was taking action on a backlog of ninety-five complaints.[130] Four stations were fined,[131] four received letters of inquiry, and the rest of the complaints were dismissed.[132] This announcement was made shortly after Alfred Sikes took over as Chairman of the FCC. Sikes had been grilled on the issue of indecency at his confirmation hearing and the Senate Commerce Committee had extracted a promise from him that he would vigorously pursue the indecency issue.[133]

This FCC announcement was followed by a year of increased enforcement of the indecency rules. Six radio stations were fined for a variety of talk, songs, and comic skits.[134] The amount of the fines ranged from $2,000 to $20,000. The Commission then released three fines against stations that broadcast Howard Stern.[135] These fines began the battle between the Commission and Stern, which would escalate over the next four years. Of the more than two million dollars in fines handed down by the end of 1997, over $1.7 million were for the broadcast of Howard Stern's morning show.

---

[128] 6 FCC Rcd 3698 (1989).
[129] 6 FCC Rcd 3698.
[130] 1989 FCC LEXIS 2317 (1989).
[131] WIOD-AM, 6 FCC Rcd 3704 (10/26/89); WZTA-FM, 6 FCC Rcd 3702 (10/26/89); KLUC-FM 6 FCC Rcd 3706 (10/26/89); and KFI-AM, 6 FCC Rcd 3699 (10/26/89).
[132] 1989 FCC LEXIS 2317. The complaints were dismissed for a number of reasons, 51 were dismissed because the broadcasts were during the safe harbor, 14 were dismissed as defective, 1 was moot because the complaint was withdrawn, and 21 were found to not be indecent.
[133] John Burgess, "FCC Presses 'Indecency' Fight; 4 Radio Stations Fined, Other Sent Letters," The Washington Post, A1.
[134] WLUP-AM, 6 FCC Rcd 3708 (11/30/89); WWWE-AM, 6 FCC Rcd 3711 (4/25/90)l KSJO-FM, 5 FCC Rcd 3821 (6/18/90); KLOL-FM, 5 FCC Rcd 6332 (10/19/90); KSD-FM, 6 FCC Rcd 3689 (9/27/90); and WFBQ-FM, 6 FCC Rcd 3692 (7/19/90).
[135] WXRK-FM, WYSP-FM, and WJFK-FM, 5 FCC Rcd 7291 (11/29/90).

The first set of fines against Stern's employer, Infinity Broadcasting, came in November of 1990. The second appeared two years later, in October of 1992. In the intervening years, five fines were issued for relatively small amounts, varying from $2,000 to $25,000.[136] Then, in October, 1992, the FCC shocked many[137] when it fined KLSX, Los Angeles $105,000 for Howard Stern's numerous violations of the indecency standard over several weeks.[138] At that point in time, this was the largest fine ever levied against a station.

The Washington Post reported that the size of the fine was an effort to slow the number of stations simulcasting Stern.[139] Soon after, the Post reported that the Commission was considering taking action against the stations that had simulcast the same broadcasts that had gotten KLSX in trouble.[140] A few weeks after that article appeared, another Post article reported that the Commission was considering even a tougher punishment.[141] Infinity was in the process of buying the Cook-Inlet group of stations and the Commission was delaying approval of the transfer. The paper reported that Commissioner James Quello said that there was "strong sentiment" at the Commission regarding delaying or even denying the purchase.[142]

On December 18, 1992, the Commission issued another record fine in the amount of $600,000; $200,000 each for three stations broadcasting Howard

---

[136] KCNA-FM, 6 FCC Rcd 2174 (4/23/91); WVIC-FM, 6 FCC Rcd 2178 (4/17/91); WYBB-FM, 7 FCC Rcd 1595 (2/14/92); KGB-FM, 7 FCC Rcd 3207 (5/26/92); and KMEL-FM, 7 FCC Rcd 4857 (7/29/92).

[137] Paul Farhi, "FCC Fines Station $105,000 Over Stern; Largest-Ever Penalty for 'Indecent' Broadcast," The Washington Post, 28 October 1992, D1.

[138] 7 FCC Rcd 7321 (1992).

[139] Jeffrey Yorke, "Stern Talk Results in Fine," The Washington Post, 27 October 1992, C7.

[140] Jeffrey Yorke, "'Smut' Inquiry Spreading; FCC Probes WJFK's Airing of 'Howard Stern Show'," The Washington Post, 3 November 1992, C7.

[141] Paul Farhi, "FCC's Stern Punishment; Radio Group to be Fined, Purchases May be Delayed," The Washington Post, 25 November 1992, E1.

[142] Farhi, "FCC's Stern Punishment," E1.

Stern.[143] The fines were for the same multiple violations of the indecency regulations that garnered the fine for KLSX. On the same day, the Commission announced that it would approve the Cook-Inlet purchase. In a concurrence, Commissioner Quello stated that it would be unfair to punish Cook-Inlet for Infinity's mistakes.[144]

In the first few months of 1993, another three stations were fined for the broadcast of indecent material. Compared to the recent $600,000 fine levied against Infinity, the fines were small; ranging from $23,750 to $33, 750.[145]

The Commission soon returned to Howard Stern. On August 12, 1993, the FCC fined KFBI-FM, Pahrump, NV, $73,750 for several broadcasts of the "Howard Stern Show."[146] Although not an Infinity station, KFBI simulcast the program. On the same day, the Commission fined four Infinity stations $125,000 each for the same set of broadcasts.[147] On February 1, 1994, KFBI-FM was fined again, this time for $37,500.[148] Again, the Commission chose to also fine four Infinity stations. This time, the fine was for $100,000 per station.[149] Thus, in six months, more than a million dollars in fines had been levied against stations broadcasting Howard Stern. Infinity Broadcasting refused to pay the fines, but it was reported that it was a making serious effort to tone down Stern's performance.[150] In the balance was another station purchase by Infinity that was being held up by the Commission.[151]

---

143 WXRK-FM, WYSP-FM, and WJFK-FM, 8 FCC Rcd 2688 (12/18/92).
144 WXRK-FM, WYSP-FM, and WJFK-FM, 8 FCC Rcd 2688, 2692.
145 WSUC-FM, 8 FCC Rcd 456 (1/1/93); WLUP-AM, 8 FCC Rcd 1266 (2/25/93); and KLOL-FM, 8 FCC Rcd 3228 (5/6/93).
146 8 FCC Rcd 6790 (1993).
147 WXRK-FM, WYSP-FM, WJFK-FM and WJFK-AM, 8 FCC Rcd 6740 (1994).
148 9 FCC Rcd 1753 (1994).
149 WXRK-FM, WYSP-FM, WJFK-FM and WJFK-AM, 9 FCC Rcd 1746 (1994).
150 Richard Harrington, "Howard Stern; All Id, No Lid; He's Raunchy and Ranting. But is He Sick or Slick?," The Washington Post, 28 October 1993, D1.
151 David S. Hilzenrath, "FCC Targets Employer of Radio 'Shock Jock;' Agency Delays Infinity Purchase of 3 Stations," The Washington Post, 1 January 1994, B1; Paul Farhi, "FCC Still

The Commission did approve that purchase in May of 1994,[152] but also levied another large fine against four Infinity stations, $50,000 per station.[153] This fine marked the last major fine issued by the Commission against Infinity. Over the next three years, fourteen more fines were issued against a variety of stations, but none for more than $12,500.[154]

Most of the fines issued between 1989 and 1997 were paid by the stations with little fuss. The last major fine issued against Infinity came in May of 1994, bringing the total amount owed by Infinity to over $1.7 million. Mel Karmazin, CEO of Infinity, had pledged all along he would not pay the fines in order to force the FCC to take him to court.[155] But 1995 brought legislation in Congress that gave Infinity pause. During the debate on what would become the Telecommunications Act of 1996, Congress removed most of the limits on the numbers of radio stations that one company could own. Infinity, the largest radio company in the United States, saw an opportunity to become even larger and thus desired a "normalized" relationship with the FCC.[156] This led to discussions of a settlement.[157]

Weighting Decision on Infinity Broadcasting's Purchase," The Washington Post, 6 January 1994, D11; and Paul Farhi, "Stern, Firm Said to Avoid Stiff Penalty," The Washington Post, 28 January 1994, G2.

[152] Jason Vest, "FCC to Fine Infinity Over Stern broadcasts; But Firm Allowed to Buy WPGC," The Washington Post, 21 May 1994, D1.

[153] WXRK-FM, WYSP-FM, WJFK-FM and WJFK-AM, 9 FCC Rcd 6442 (1994).

[154] KFMH-FM, 9 FCC Rcd 1681 (4/1/94); KNON-FM, 9 FCC Rcd 1679 (4/1/94); KKLZ-FM, 9 FCC Rcd 4454 (8/29/94); WWST-FM, 9 FCC Rcd 4871 (9/14/94); WGRF-FM, 10 FCC Rcd 5149 (9/5/95); WBZU-FM, 11 FCC Rcd 13214 (10/15/96); WVIC-FM, 11 FCC Rcd 12744 (10/4/96); KTFM-FM, 1996 FCC LEXIS 6238 (11/12/96); WEZB-FM, 12 FCC Rcd 4147 (4/8/97); WCMF-AM & FM, 12 FCC Rcd 8282 (6/9/97); WXRK-FM, 12 FCC Rcd 8274 (6/24/97); WEBN-FM, 1997 FCC LEXIS 3207 (6/24/97); WFXR-TV, 12 FCC Rcd 8277(6/24/97); and KUPD-FM, 1997 FCC LEXIS 7041 (12/17/97).

[155] Paul Farhi, "Bad Taste, Good Business; To His Employer, Howard Stern Easily Passes a Classic Cost-Benefit Test," The Washington Post, 27 March 1994, H1.

[156] Paul Farhi, "Stern 'Indecency' Case Settled; After 7-year Fight with FCC, Broadcasting Firm to Pay $1.7 Million," The Washington Post, 2 September 1995, F1.

[157] Evergreen Media Corporation had already settled with the FCC for significantly less than it owed. For a good examination of the settlements, see Michelle Ballard and Milagros Rivera-

In September of 1995, the Commission announced that it had reached an agreement with Infinity Broadcasting.[158] In exchange for a $1.71 million contribution to the U.S. Treasury, all indecency fines pending against Infinity's stations would be vacated. Infinity admitted no guilt. In addition, any future fines for indecency would be treated as a first offense. This swept the record clean, allowing Infinity to embark on a buying spree that ended in a merger with Westinghouse Electric, owner of CBS.[159]

Summary

This chapter presented the history of indecency regulation from the 1962 Palmetto decision until the end the Hundt Commission in December of 1997. The thirty-five year span saw the early attempts at defining indecency language as something separate from obscenity. This distinction is critical, since obscenity is illegal in this country, while indecency is protected by the First Amendment. Indecency can be regulated, but it can not be banned outright.

The earliest attempts at regulation included a variety of stations and programming. Charlie Walker's down-home, off-color humor, while not the official reason why Palmetto Broadcasting lost its license in 1962, was the reason why the station was investigated in the first place. In 1964, 1965, and 1969, the Pacifica Foundation's avant-guard programming brought its stations to the FCC's attention. Finally, a thirty-hour autobiography on tape of a local reverend almost lost the Jack Straw Memorial Foundation its license for KRAB-FM.

Sanchez, "Settlement: FCC's Newest Strategy to Address Indecency?," Communications and the Law 18:4 (1996): 1-27.

[158] 10 FCC Rcd 12245 (1995).

[159] Paul Farhi, "Top 2 Radio Station Operators to Merge in $4.9 Billion Deal," The Washington Post, 21 June 1996, A1.

In the early 1970s, the FCC made its first forays into fining stations for indecency, seeking judicial review of its definition of indecency. The Commission issue a $100 fine to one station, WUHY-FM, for the broadcast of a profanity-filled interview with Jerry Garcia. Sonderling Broadcasting's WGLD-FM, received a $2,000 fine for a call-in program known as "Topless Radio." Both WUHY-FM and WGLD-FM paid the fines and refused to seek judicial review. But FCC's decision that the Pacifica Foundation's broadcast of the George Carlin monologue, "Seven Filthy Words" was indecent gave the Commission its first chance at a judicial review.

The United States Supreme Court found that the monologue was indecent "as broadcast." This narrow decision led the Commission to enforce a ban on only the seven words at issue in the Pacifica decision, and only when they were used repeatedly before ten p.m. This was the situation for nine years.

In April, 1987, the FCC issued three decisions that served to expand the FCC's definition of indecency. The Commission now claimed that innuendo and double entendre would be considered actionable, even when the seven filthy words were not used. In addition, the FCC stated that the ten p.m. safe harbor was no longer valid.

These decisions sparked two different chains of events. The first was eight years of litigation over the parameters of the safe harbor. The second was the more than two million dollars in fines issued against Howard Stern and others. The litigation over the safe harbor resulted in the same safe harbor, ten p.m. to six p.m., that existed before the litigation started. The fines have mostly been paid by the licensees. The largest block of fines, $1.71 million against Infinity Broadcasting, was paid in a settlement that admitted no wrong-doing on the part of Infinity, Howard Stern's boss.

This chapter has shown that the history of the regulation of indecency is complex and has passed through many phases. The next chapter examines the history and goals of the American Family Association and Morality in Media before moving on to the presentation of the findings of this research.

Chapter 4
Morality in Media and the American Family Association

This chapter outlines the history, goals, and accomplishments of Morality in Media (MIM) and the American Family Association (AFA). Using information from the groups themselves and major media sources, this chapter attempts to create a snap shot of both groups. The chapter serves two purposes. First, this history, like the previous chapter, provides additional context for the findings of this research. Second, this chapter presents the media perception of the groups' accomplishments in the area of the regulation of indecency. A comparison between that perception and what can be documented by the research could prove informative.

Morality in Media

The seeds for Morality in Media were planted in 1962. Father Morton A. Hill, S.J. was a parish priest at the St. Ignatius Loyola Roman Catholic Church in Manhattan.[1] One day, his superior requested that he look into a situation at the parish elementary school.[2] A mother had complained that sadomasochistic

---

[1] "The Rev. Morton Hill; Led Pornography Foes," The New York Times, 6 November 1985, D27.; and Morality in Media. "Morality in Media Homepage." [http://pw2.netcom.com/~mimnyc/index.html]. June, 1998.

[2] "The Rev. Morton Hill; Led Pornography Foes," D27 and MIM web page.

magazines were circulating among the sixth-grade boys.[3] That request led to the organization of a community campaign against pornography, "Operation Yorkville."[4] As the group began to accumulate knowledge about the problems of obscenity and children and the obscenity laws on the books, requests for information and speakers began to come in from churches and civic groups around the New York-New Jersey-Connecticut area.[5] In response to the growing interest, Morality in Media was organized in 1968 with Father Hill as president.[6]

According its web site, MIM's mission is to use "its knowledge of the law and the vigorous involvement of informed citizens to address these pressing moral and cultural problems:"[7]

1. The exploitation of obscenity in the marketplace; and
2. The erosion of decency standards in the media.[8]

The methods that the group has used over the years to achieve that mission have varied. The next two sections detail some of the accomplishments and failures of the group. The first section looks briefly at MIM's actions on such topics as pornography, talk shows, and the v-chip. The second section deals exclusively with the issue of MIM's actions involving the regulation of broadcast indecency.

Pornography and Other Concerns

Shortly after MIM was founded in 1968, President Lyndon Johnson appointed Father Hill to the Commission on Obscenity and Pornography, a group

[3] "The Rev. Morton Hill; Led Pornography Foes," D27 and MIM web page.
[4] "The Rev. Morton Hill; Led Pornography Foes," D27 and MIM web page.
[5] MIM web page.
[6] "The Rev. Morton Hill; Led Pornography Foes," D27 and MIM web page
[7] MIM web page.
[8] MIM web page.

that Johnson assembled to determine whether the country's obscenity laws should be eliminated.[9] The majority of the Commission concluded that obscenity laws should be repealed on the grounds that pornography was harmless.[10] Father Hill, along with the other clergyman on the Commission, Dr. Winfrey C. Linker, disagreed and issued the Hill-Link Minority Report. Congress rejected the majority report and Representative Dulski placed the Hill-Link Report into the Congressional Record.[11]

Father Hill's appointment to the Pornography Commission marked the beginning of a long involvement in the regulation of obscenity and pornography by Morality in Media. Soon after the Pornography Commission issued its report, Father Hill began to seek federal funding for the creation of a clearinghouse of information on the law of obscenity to aid prosecutors and others interested in enforcing the legal restrictions on obscenity.[12] The center was opened in early 1972 on the campus of the California Lutheran College.[13] After federal funding was cut off in 1975,[14] the center re-opened with the help of private funds as the National Obscenity Law Center in New York in 1976.[15] The Center is still active.

In 1983, Father Hill and a coalition of religious and political leaders met with President Ronald Reagan to ask him to increase the government's efforts against illegal pornography.[16] White House aide Morton Backwell reported that

---

[9] "Rev. Morton Hill, 68, Pornography Opponent," Chicago Tribune, 7 November 1985, Chicagoland 10 and MIM web page.

[10] "Pornography Opponent," 10 and MIM web page.

[11] 91 Cong. Rec. 34215 (1970); "Pornography Opponent," 10; and MIM web page.

[12] MIM web site.

[13] MIM web site.

[14] A California attorney succeeded getting funding cut off on the grounds that since Cal Lutheran was a religious college, the center represented a violation of the separation of church and state.

[15] "National Obscenity Law Center Created," The New York Times, 2 September 1976, 33; "Pornography Opponent," 10; and MIM web site.

[16] "President Reagan," Facts on File World Digest, 3 June 1983, 408 G2 and David Hoffman, "Reagan Hears Pleas to Battle Pornography," The Washington Post, 29 March 1983, A5.

the president had been "very receptive" to the groups concerns.[17] Soon after that meeting, Reagan formed the Working Group on Pornography and invited Father Hill to participate.[18] One of the items on Father Hill's agenda for the Working Group was the inclusion of obscenity in the Federal Racketeer Influenced and Corrupt Organizations Law (RICO), which would allow the Justice Department to confiscate the assets of a business convicted under the statute.[19] Not long after, President Reagan signed the Comprehensive Crime Control Act into law, which included the RICO/pornography amendment.[20]

The local chapters of MIM have also worked with the government to aid in the prosecution of obscenity.[21] Some chapters have worked with district attorneys and police to pressure stores to take material off the shelves;[22] others have lobbied to change local zoning laws to make it harder for stores selling pornographic material to open in the first place.[23] Some groups go so far as to hold monthly meetings with the local district attorney in an effort to keep obscene material out of video and book stores.[24] The Massachusetts chapter even aided in the drafting of new obscenity laws.[25]

Both the national organization and the local chapters are also concerned with creating public awareness. MIM sponsors such events as Pornography Awareness Week,[26] the White Ribbons Against Pornography campaign,[27] and the

---

[17] Hoffman, A5.
[18] "Pornography Opponent," 10 and MIM web site.
[19] "Pornography Opponent," 10.
[20] "Pornography Opponent," 10.
[21] Judy Chicurel, "Morality in Media Takes on Adult Stores," The New York Times, 17 June 1990, 12LI -1.
[22] Colleen McMillar, "Adult Video Tougher to Find With New Laws," The Times-Picayune, 25 January 1993, B2 and Chicurel, 12LI-1.
[23] Chicurel, 12LI-1.
[24] Suzanne Billelo, "Her Target: Pornography," Newsday, 19 July 1989, 2.
[25] Patty Hartigan, "Group Takes on Obscenity Law," The Boston Globe, 8 March 1991, Arts & Film 29.
[26] Blanch Hatch, "Fight Pornography," Chicago Daily Herald, 26 October 1997, 16.

annual Turn Off the TV Day.[28] The group also holds public forums around the country to educate people about the dangers of pornography and the laws that govern its distribution.[29] Local chapters often use picket lines for a dual purpose: encouraging the stores to take pornography off the shelves and educating the shoppers.[30]

MIM has spoken out against dial-a-porn, pornography on cable and the Internet, and the v-chip ratings system.[31] It has opposed the judicial appointment of a lawyer who had defended owners of adult bookstores. The group has also been critical of the homosexual main character on the television show, "Ellen,"[32] Calvin Klein ads that used young-looking models in seductive poses,[33] and the portrayal of sex between a man and a twelve-year-old girl in the 1998 film version of Lolita.[34] In 1996, MIM took on the television talk shows, like "Jerry Springer" and "Ricki Lake," monitoring each program for content and advertisers in the

---

[27] "Anti-Porn Campaign is Announced by Morality in Media," The Providence Journal-Bulletin, 27 October 1994, 19D.

[28] Mark Byers, "Saturday Commentary: Accentuate the Positive in TV; 'Media Watchdogs' Taking Wrong Approach in Efforts to Enforce Morality in Programming," The Daily News of Los Angeles, 14 February 1998, N24; Kathryn Rogers, "'Morality in Media' Targets TV; Fight 'Sleaze' by Turning Off Sets All Day on Friday, Group Urges," St. Louis Dispatch, 10 February 1994, 4A; Dennis McDougal, "TV Boycott Fails to Dent Tuesday Ratings," Los Angeles Times, 31 October 1991, F5; and Valerie Takahama, "Sex, Violence; Thousands of Angry Viewers Join 'Turn Off TV Day'," The Orange County Register, 30 October 1991, B7.

[29] Jerry Miller, "Pornography Assailed by Morality in Media President at Forum," The Union Leader, 26 July 1993, 6.

[30] Chicurel, 12LI-1

[31] M. L. Lyke, "Online Smut: Too Easy for Kids to Find?; Pornography: An Innocent Search Can Lead Children to X-Rated Web Sites," The Baltimore Sun, 4 May 1998, 3C; Barbara O'Brien, "Spice Fare is Obscene, Group Told; Leader of Morality in Media Asks Action," The Buffalo News, 28 October 1993, Local Page; Edmund L. Andrews, "2 Views of Decency," The New York Times, 28 December 1992, A12; and Ray Richmond, "Morality in Media Rips TV Rating Plan," Daily Variety, 5 December 1996, 5.

[32] "TV's Ellen Controversy Expected to Continue, Actress to be on News Show Friday," The Dallas Morning News, 25 April 1997, 4B.

[33] Pierre Thomas and Paul Farhi, "Calvin Klein Ads Cleared," The Washington Post, 16 November 1995, D7.

[34] Andrea Peyser, "Obscenity of Censors Taints Art of 'Lolita'," The New York Post, 7 May 1998, 24.

February and November sweeps week.[35] The group then publicized the levels of violence and sexual content in the programs, and listed the advertisers who sponsored the programs.[36] The current president, Robert Peters, has been highly critical of "Jerry Springer," and the host's refusal to tone down the broadcast.[37]

As this section has shown, MIM has been active throughout the years in many ways on the issue of pornography and obscenity in this country. Indecency on the broadcast media has also been a major concern and area of activity for the group. The next section details MIM's efforts in the regulation of broadcast indecency.

Broadcast Indecency

According to its general counsel, Paul McGeady, Morality in Media has no interest in silencing ideas.[38] MIM's sole concern is keeping obscenity and indecency from the public airwaves. "They don't belong to any one person. . . . The airwaves belong to the public" according to McGeady.[39] Current MIM president Robert Peters has likened indecency on the public airwaves to nudity on a public street, declaring it unacceptable.[40] For this reason, MIM has chosen to pursue tough enforcement of the regulations governing broadcast indecency.[41]

Morality in Media was involved in the FCC's regulation of indecency from almost the beginning. John Douglas, the man who sent the complaint about the Pacifica broadcast of George Carlin's monologue to the FCC, was a member of

---

[35] Joe Flint, "Survey Finds Less Raciness," Daily Variety, 26 December 1996, 1.
[36] Flint, 1.
[37] Tracy Conner, "Jerry Vows He'll Go Down Fighting; Balks at Talk of Easing Up on Sleaze," The New York Post, 2 May 1998, 4.
[38] Dennis McDougal, "Obscenity Issue Still Unresolved," Los Angeles Times, 4 January 1988, 6-1.
[39] McDougal, "Obscenity Issue," 6-1.
[40] Robert W. Peters, "Information Superhighway or Technological Sewer: What Will It Be?," Federal Communication Law Journal 47:December (1994): 333-338.
[41] Peters, 337.

the group's national planning board.[42] Morality in Media also submitted an amicus brief to the Supreme Court on behalf of the FCC in the Pacifica case.[43] Shortly after the Pacifica decision, MIM petitioned the FCC to deny the renewal of license to WGBH-TV, Boston on the grounds of the broadcast of indecent material. The petition failed, and the decision was used by the FCC to announce its intention to apply the Supreme Court's decision narrowly.[44]

The 1978 WGBH decision marked the beginning of nearly a decade of non-enforcement of the indecency regulations by the Commission. But in April, 1987, the Commission announced that it would more actively enforce the indecency restrictions, and would consider more than just the seven words in question in Pacifica as a measure of indecency. Shortly before the decisions were announced, Morality in Media had threatened to picket the FCC's building at 1919 M Street in Washington, D.C. because of the inaction on indecency.[45] MIM had also met with the Commissioners and their staff about more actively enforcing the indecency policy.[46] In addition, MIM advised a Philadelphia woman on how to prepare one of the complaints that sparked the 1987 April Trio decisions.[47] Because of all this, many media reports of the FCC's actions placed responsibility squarely at the feet of Morality in Media.[48]

---

[42] Steve Weinstein, "How 'Jerker' Helped Ignite Obscenity Debate; Comedian Carlin has a Few Choice Words for Media Watchdogs," Los Angeles Times, 18 August 1987, 6-1; Lois P. Sheinfeld, "FCC Doublespeak," Film Comment, September/October, 87-90; and the MIM web site.

[43] Warren Weaver, "Justice Department Reverses Stance on Indecency," The New York Times, 1 April 1978, 14.

[44] "FCC Censorship Role Rejected," Facts on File World Digest, 4 August 1978, 599 E1.

[45] John Crigler and William J. Byrnes, "Decency Redux: The Curious History of the New FCC Broadcast Indecency Policy," Catholic University Law Review 38:Winter (1989): 329-363; and MIM web site.

[46] Crigler and MIM web site.

[47] Alex S. Jones, "FCC Studies 'Indecency' on Radio," The New York Times, 22 November 1986, 9.

[48] Allan Parachini and Dennis McDougal, "Art in the Eighties; Censorship: A Decade of Tighter Control of the Arts," Los Angeles Times, 25 December 1989, F1; Dennis McDougal, "FCC Won't Back Off From April Indecency Ruling; More Explicit Programming After Midnight," Los

Not only did the media attribute the tougher restrictions to MIM, but both Commissioner James Quello and Chairman Mark Fowler cited outside pressure on the Commission as reason for the change. Quello stated that "the commission is caught in a crossfire" between First Amendment advocates and a "growing public outcry for action against indecency on the air."[49] Fowler reported that the pressure from Congress and others to do something about indecency was "intense," and that the April Trio decisions were an attempt to relieve that pressure.[50]

Many groups petitioned the FCC for reconsideration of the April decision to expand the indecency regulation. Among them was Morality in Media, who asked the Commission to ban indecency twenty-four hours a day.[51] That petition failed to garner the Commission's support and MIM was often quoted as believing the FCC was not going far enough in its regulation of indecency.[52] General Counsel Paul McGeady characterized the FCC's actions as "pushing the pig into the parlors of millions of American homes after midnight."[53]

Morality in Media did not stop with the April 1987 decisions in its quest to clear up the broadcast airwaves. MIM has consistently opposed the concept of any safe harbor of the broadcast of indecent material. Media reports of the time also attributed Senator Jesse Helms' amendment that mandated a twenty-

---

Angeles Times, 25 November 1987, 6-1; Mark Conrad, "With a New President Comes a New FCC Agenda," New York Law Journal January 15 (1993): 5; Paul Farhi, "Stern 'Indecency' Case Settled; After 7-year Fight with FCC, Broadcasting Firm to Pay $1.7 Million," The Washington Post, 2 September 1995, F1; and Jones, 9.

[49] Dennis McDougal, "Radio Daze: FCC Moves Indecency Issue to Front Burner," Los Angeles Times, 17 August 1987, 6-1.

[50] Paul Farhi, "War of the Words," The Washington Post, 21 May 1995, W12.

[51] "FCC Indecency Ban Goes to Court," Broadcasting, 9 January 1989, 70.

[52] "Filtering Airwaves for Indecency," The New York Times, 1 November 1987, 65 and Dennis McDougal, "At Issue: 'Indecency' Still Murky Issue," Los Angeles Times, 19 February 1988, Part 6-1.

four hour ban on indecency to pressure from groups like Morality in Media.[54] In line with MIM's public awareness program, many of the complaints that sparked indecency fines came from people who were aided and educated by the group.[55]

Morality in Media has been active in the legal drive to remove indecent and obscene material from television, cable, the Internet, telephones, video stores, and newsstands. One past president of the group, Joseph C. Reilly, Jr., described the goal of the organization as working "within the Constitution to have obscenity laws that are effective and have them enforced."[56] This section has shown what the organization has done to further that goal. The next section presents the activities of the American Family Association.

American Family Association

The February 28, 1995, edition of the trade publication Advertising Age listed the fifty people who "Made TV's Landscape." Included among such luminaries as Johnny Carson, Peggy Charren, Newton Minow, and William Paley, was the Reverend Donald Wildmon of the American Family Association.[57] Likewise, a San Diego Union-Tribune article about pressure groups who sought to influence television included AFA, and described Wildmon as "high-profile."[58] The Los Angeles Times described AFA as the most "broadly influential" pressure

---

[53] Irvin Molotsky, "FCC Rules on Indecent Programming," The New York Times, 25 November 1987, C25 and John Burgess, "FCC to Permit 'Indecency' at Certain Times," The Washington Post, 25 November 1987, E1.

[54] Dennis McDougal, "U.S. Likened to Iran on Free Speech," The Record, 29 March 1989, E16.

[55] Joseph J. Reilly, "Keep the Airwaves Clean," Newsday, 4 February 1990, 2; Paul D. Colford, "Another Stern Challenge," Newsday, 31 January 1990, 7; Dennis McDougal, "FCC Versus Howard Stern: Agency's 'Indecency' Ruling Hasn't Stopped N.Y. Deejay," Los Angeles Times, 19 August 1987, 6-1; and "Racy DJ Gets WXRK in Trouble," The Record, 18 November 1986, A1.

[56] Renee Graham, "Morality's Defenders or Freedom's Enemies?," The Boston Globe, 6 August 1990, Metro/Region 13.

[57] "50 Who Made TV's Landscape; Honed by Pioneers and Visionaries," Advertising Age, 28 February 1995, 44.

group of the 1980s, "a role-player--center stage or behind the scenes--in virtually every free expression controversy of the last five years."[59] While the networks deny that Wildmon has had any effect on programming,[60] many advertising executives say otherwise,[61] claiming he has "deeply shaken the advertising world."[62]

The American Family Association began life as the National Federation for Decency. During the 1976 Christmas holidays, a United Methodist minister named Donald Wildmon sat down to watch television with his children.[63] As the oft-told story goes, the first program they saw was a scene of adultery. He asked the children to change the channel and on the next program, one man called another an "s.o.b." Again, he asked the children to change the channel. This time, they saw a man beating another man with a hammer. He asked the children to turn the television off.[64] Not too long after that, the Rev. Wildmon urged his congregation to turn their televisions off for a week as a protest. The story was picked up in the national media and Wildmon discovered that many people were equally outraged by the state of television. The National Federation of Decency was organized in 1977.[65]

---

[58] Joe Stein, "A Rundown of Pressure Groups Who Seek to Influence TV," The San Diego Union-Tribune, 14 July 1989, C-15.

[59] Allan Parachini and Dennis McDougal, "Censorship and the Arts Reach Boiling Point," Los Angeles Times, 18 June 1990, F1.

[60] Mary T. Schmich, "The Gospel on Trash TV; Rev. Donald Wildmon Feels Called to Make the Networks Pay," Chicago Tribune, 22 May 1989, Tempo 1.

[61] Don Kowet, "The 'Righteous Indignation' of Donald Wildmon; How a Mississippi Minister Terrorizes the TV Networks," The Washington Times, 12 July 1989, E1.

[62] Schmich, Tempo 1 and American Family Association. "American Family Association Homepage." [http://www.afa.net/afa_bro.htm]. June, 1998.

[63] Schmich, Tempo 1 and AFA web site.

[64] Schmich, Tempo 1 and AFA web site.

[65] James Cox, "Rev. Donald Wildmon; Mississippi Minister Takes on TV Networks," USA Today, 17 July 1989, 6B; Schmich, Tempo 1; and AFA web site.

The National Federation for Decency became the American Family Association in 1988.[66] At the same time, Wildmon has also served as the head of two other coalitions aimed at cleaning up television: the now-defunct Coalition for Better Television (CBTV) with Moral Majority's Jerry Falwell[67] and the still-active Christian Leaders for Responsible Television (CLeaR-TV).[68] Wildmon is at the center of all these groups, continuously preaching that television's "exploitation of sexuality and violence, its use of language, its stereotyping of given groups--particularly Christians--has had a negative, destructive influence on our society."[69]

The American Family Association claims upwards of 500 state and local chapters,[70] and the AFA Journal has a reported circulation of nearly 400,000.[71] AFA also has a law center dedicated to defending the civil rights of Christians around the country.[72] AFA's outreach to the community also include the American Family Radio network,[73] and a pornography addiction help-line.[74]

---

[66] AFA web site. For the sake of clarity, the group is identified as the American Family Association for the entirety of this history. Any happening before 1988 is assumed to be the National Federation for Decency. If the group is CLeaR-TV or CBTV, they are identified as such. There has never been a publicly-stated reason why the group changed its name to the American Family Association.

[67] Megan Rosenfeld, "The Battle for Prime-Time Decency; The National Federal for Decency's Battle with Prime-Time Television," The Washington Post, 3 February 1981, B1 and Joel Swerdlow, "The Great American Crusade in Televisionland," The Washington Post, 7 June 1981, K1.

[68] Barbara Carton, "Lashing Back at TV Sleaze; Outraged Viewers Gird to Boycott Advertisers," The Boston Globe, 23 April 1989, A1 and AFA web site.

[69] Cox, 6B.

[70] Lois M. Rogers, "Events to Celebrate National Prayer Day," Asbury Park Press, 1 May 1996, B5 and Lois M. Rogers, "Return to Family Values Waretown Man's Mission," Asbury Park Press, 5 July 1995, G10.

[71] Michael J. McManus, "Organization Flexes Muscle Against Porn with Journal," The Fresno Bee, 19 April 1997, C7.

[72] Rogers, "Return to Family Values," G-10.

[73] Erwin Seba, "Smut-Fighter Gaining Access to Wichita with Station Buy," Wichita Business Journal, 10 June 1994, 1.

[74] Mike Harden, "Pornography Lurks Almost Everywhere in Watchdog's Eyes," The Columbus Dispatch, 14 January 1998, 1E.

The American Family Association has been active in trying to clean up the media for more than twenty years. During that time, the group has dealt with decency issues in television, radio, magazines, cable, and convenience stores. A later section of this chapter documents AFA's involvement in broadcast indecency. But, before focusing on the indecency issue, the next section presents some of the other issues that AFA has confronted.

Pornography and Other Concerns

One of AFA's earliest concerns was mainstream businesses that sold adult material. AFA is widely credited with convincing the Southland Corporation to remove adult magazines like Playboy and Penthouse from the shelves of its 7-Eleven stores.[75] While the company did not publicly acknowledge AFA's role, Southland Vice President Allen Liles stated that the 7-Eleven stores were trying to change their crime-prone image and the last thing that the company needed was a religious picket that associated porn with crime.[76] According to Liles, "We are a neighborhood store. . . . We want to be a good neighbor."[77]

The same tactics did not, however, convince the Circle K stores to follow suit.[78] In 1989, AFA organized a nation-wide picket of the stores, asking them to remove the magazines.[79] After six years of trying to no avail, the group

[75] Richard Louv, "In Moral Marketing, Statistics Don't Count for Much," The San Diego Union-Tribune, 11 May 1986, A-3; Betty Beard, "New Bid for Circle K Boycott; Religious Group Wants Chain to Halt Sales of 'Porn'," The Arizona Republic, 8 November 1995, A15; and Arlena Sawyers, "Group Launches Boycott of Chrysler, Cites Playboy Ads," Automotive News, 14 January 1991, 3.
[76] Louv, A-3.
[77] Louv, A-3.
[78] Mark Monday, "Adult-Magazine Sales Stir Handful of Pickets at 2 South County Stores," The San Diego Union-Tribune, 20 April 1989, B-18 and Beard, A15
[79] Monday, B-18.

announced a boycott of Circle K in 1995.[80] Circle K still refuses to remove the magazines, citing its First Amendment rights to sell the material.[81]

AFA did have some success with the Holiday Inn chain. In 1987, ten of the chain's motels in Florida, Pennsylvania, North Carolina, and Texas were picketed for allowing guests to watch pornographic movies in their rooms.[82] The July 1988 AFA Journal reported that 200 Holiday Inns notified AFA that they did not or would no longer carry the movies.[83]

Other mainstream stores have been AFA targets. Kmart came under attack because its subsidiary, Waldenbooks, carried adult magazines. Four years after the boycott began, The Los Angeles Times reported Kmart's poor performance in its eighth quarterly report in a row.[84] Blockbuster drew AFA's ire because the Blockbuster Music stores were carrying R-rated Playboy videos.[85] A final example of AFA's attempt to keep mainstream business away from pornography was the AFA boycott of Chrysler for running an advertisement in Playboy.[86]

A wide range of television, movies, and even cartoons have warranted the attention of the American Family Association. The organization has had some successes and some failures in its attempts to clean up the media through boycotts. In some cases, AFA pressured advertisers and advertising agencies directly.[87] In others, the organization dealt with the program producers.

---

[80] Beard, A15.
[81] Beard, A15.
[82] "The Nation," Los Angeles Times, 19 April 1987, 2.
[83] "Pressure Group Claims Success," St. Petersburg Times, 9 July 1998, 7E.
[84] Robert V. Nugent, "Kmart's Earnings," Los Angeles Times, 26 March 1995, D2. In response to the efforts against Kmart by AFA's Florida chapter, Waldenbooks and Playboy, among others, filed a racketeering suit against the organization. See "Suit Seeks to Halt Campaign Against 'Adult' Magazine Sales," St. Louis Post-Dispatch, 2 November 1989, 15A and Donald E. Wildmon, "Protect the Right to Boycott Pornography," USA Today, 25 April 1990, 10A.
[85] "Group Protests Playboy Videos," The Orlando Sentinel, 25 October 1994, C3.
[86] Sawyers, 3.
[87] Estelle Lander, "Advertisers Get the Squeeze," New York Newsday, 17 April 1989, 1; Michael Lev, "A Conservative Group Sends Boycott Warning," The New York Times, 15 July 1991, D9; and Stuart Elliot, "Networks are Putting the Pressure on Pressure Groups," The New York Times,

Wildmon, with his various groups, CBTV, CLeaR-TV, and AFA, has organized a number of monitoring campaigns designed to measure the amounts of sex and violence in prime time television in order to determine whom to boycott.[88]

Taking issue with presentations of sex, violence, and non-traditional lifestyles, the American Family Association has used advertiser boycotts to challenge television shows like "Saturday Night Live,"[89] "NYPD Blue,"[90] "Brooklyn South,"[91] "Ellen,"[92] "Murphy Brown,"[93] and "Love, Sidney."[94] AFA

---

1 August 1991, D17. AFA has often launched a campaign against a specific company because of their overall media spending. Some of the companies targeted have been Sears (Don Wildmon, "Book Excerpt: 'Don Wildmon'," Electronic Media, 8 January 1990, 89.); Pepsi (Ray Richmond, "When Consumers Talk, Sponsors Listen," The Orange County Register, 9 April 1989, L28.); and Unilever (Daniel Jeffreys, "When a Wildmon Wreaks Havoc; The White Knight of American Family Values Knows No Limits When Pitted Against Big Business," The Independent, 27 July 1995, Life 6; Gary Levin, "Wildmon Boycott Sparks Unilever Second Thoughts," Daily Variety, 3 July 1995, 3; Daniel Jeffreys, "Stateside," The Independent, 20 June 1995, 16; and "Christian Group Calls for Boycott of Unilever," Los Angeles Times, 13 June 1995, D3.).

[88]AFA: "Watchdog group: Violence on TV Rises Significantly," The Des Moines Register, 6 September 1995, 5; CLeaR-TV: Nathan Cobb, "Prime Time Sex; What's Most Surprising About the Increasing Sexual Content of Network TV is that Anyone is Surprised by it at All," The Boston Globe, 30 April 1989, Magazine 20 and Barbara Carton, "Lashing Back at TV Sleaze; Outraged Viewers Gird to Boycott Advertisers," The Boston Globe, 23 April 1989, A1; and CBTV: "Group to Gauge TV Smut, Seek Sponsor Boycotts," The Christian Science Monitor, 3 February 1981, 2; Tony Schwartz, "400 Rightist Groups in National Coalition to Start Boycott of TV; Wildmon Sponsors This Week," The New York Times, 22 January 1981, A12; Joseph B. Treaster, "TV Advertisers Meet Coalition in Effort to Avoid Boycott," The New York Times, 26 June 1981, A10; Megan Rosenfeld, "The Battle for Prime-Time Decency; The National Federal for Decency's Battle with Prime-Time Television," The Washington Post, 3 February 1981, B1; and Joel Swerdlow, "The Great American Crusade in Televisionland," The Washington Post, 7 June 1981, K1.

[89] Kathleen O'Steen, "Wildmon Spends Big Ad Bucks Against H'Wood," Daily Variety, 2 December 1992, 8; Eleanor Blau, "Domino's Pulls 'Saturday Night' Ads," The New York Times, 11 April 1989, D25; and "Ralston in 'Saturday Night' Flap," St. Louis Post-Dispatch, 17 March 1989, 13D.

[90] Tom Walter, "TV Strikes Gold with 'Crude'," The Commercial Appeal, 8 March 1998, E1; Nancy Millman, "Missing the Mark; Wildmon's Battle with TV a Big Zero, Experts Say," Chicago Tribune, 12 April 1994, Tempo 2; and Stuart Elliot, "A Hit Prime-Time Show Without Most Mainstream Advertisers? Dial 'NYPD Blue'," The New York Times, 2 November 1993, D20.

[91] Christopher Stern, "Content Controversy Goes 'South'," Variety, 18 August 1997, 21.

[92] John Hiscock, "Ellen is Out of the Closet and Out of the Door," The Daily Telegraph, 25 April 1998, 3.

[93] Thomas Tyrer, "'Murphy' Sponsors Targets for Boycott," Electronic Media, 27 July 1992, 4 and "Ad Boycott Aimed at Murphy Brown," The Record, 23 July 1992, C16.

tried unsuccessfully to block the broadcast of two made-for-TV movies involving abortion: NBC's Roe v. Wade[95] and CBS's Absolute Strangers[96] by encouraging the sponsors to pull out of the broadcasts or face a boycott.

Other organizations, people, and programs that have drawn AFA's attention have included PBS, for presenting what AFA considers homosexual propaganda;[97] musician and self-proclaimed Satanist Marilyn Manson;[98] Calvin Klein, for running advertisements featuring young-looking models in seductive poses;[99] and libraries for having the Howard Stern book, Miss America, on its shelves.[100] The group has also protested material containing what it considers negative religious portrayals, including movies like The Last Temptation of Christ[101] and Priest[102] and the comic strip Bloom County, which named a religious character Edith Dreck.[103]

AFA has had some success in the areas of children's media. The group's threatened boycott convinced the Matchbox toy company to cancel production on

---

[94] Tom Shales, "Tony Randall for the Defense; The Series and the Fury; A Furor Over NBC's New 'Love, Sidney'," The Washington Post, 7 July 1981, C1.

[95] Diane Mermigas, "'Roe' Loses Ads; NBC Stands Firm," Electronic Media, 15 May 1989, 3 and Jeremy Gerard, "Enough Ads are Expected for NBC's Abortion Film," The New York Times, 12 May 1989, D15.

[96] Verne Gay, "Group Targets 'Absolute Strangers'," Newsday, 18 March 1991, 53.

[97] John Carman, "Righteous Reverend Writes Again," The San Francisco Chronicle, 4 April 1994, E1.

[98] Ben Werner, "The Adventures of Ozzy and Marilyn," The Orange County Register, 27 June 1997, F10.

[99] Pat Sloan and Jennifer DeCoursey, "Klein's Risqué Jean Ads Dodge Kiddie Porn Rap from the Feds," Advertising Age, 20 November 1995, 25; "New York Report," WWD, 2 November 1995, 6; and Andrea Sachs, "Kiddie Porn or Bad Taste?; AFA's Trueman Says Jeans Ads Cross Legal Line," Advertising Age, 18 September 1995, 52.

[100] Jim Mallory, "Group Threatens Suit to Force Book's Removal," The Denver Post, 30 April 1997, B-3.

[101] "Wildmon Threatens Boycott over 'Temptation'," The San Diego Union-Tribune, 15 July 1988, C-11.

[102] Victor Volland, "Video Stores have 'Priest'; Groups Protest," St. Louis Post-Dispatch, 27 January 1996, 5D.

[103] "Bloom County Comic Strip Angers Religious Leader," The San Diego Union-Tribune, 9 July 1987, A-11.

a Freddy Krueger doll, based on the Nightmare on Elm Street horror movies.[104] AFA also had a hand in CBS's decision not to air a cartoon series based on the Garbage Pail Kids trading cards.[105] A final example of AFA's involvement in children's media is involves Mighty Mouse and illegal drugs.[106] In an episode aired in 1988, Mighty Mouse was seen inhaling a "powdery white substance."[107] The substance, according to Wildmon, was cocaine.[108] After resisting for months, CBS cut three and a half seconds from the episode.[109]

AFA has also been active in boycotting any company that takes what it deems a pro-homosexual position. The Walt Disney Company has been a target of an AFA boycott[110] for its decision to extend insurance benefits to employee's homosexual partners and allowing a "Gay Day" in the theme parks.[111] One chapter, American Family Association of Texas, has even pushed for state officials to sell $27 million in Disney stock held by its school trust fund.[112] AFA has also boycotted Levi Strauss for its decision to stop supporting the Boy Scouts because of the Scouts refusal to allow homosexuals to be troop leaders.[113]

---

[104] "Saturday Ticker," Chicago Tribune, 21 October 1989, Business 8.
[105] "Newsbites," The Orange County Register, 17 September 1987, K2.
[106] Craig Wolff, "Mighty Mouse Flying High on Flowers," The New York Times, 26 July 1988, B1 and Henry Allen, "The Might Controversy; Rodent Hero Accused of Sniffing Cocaine.," The Washington Post, 10 June 1988, D1.
[107] Wolff, B1.
[108] Wolff, B1.
[109] Wolff, B1.
[110] AFA also considers Disney's support of Ellen (ABC subsidiary) and Howard Stern (E! channel subsidiary) anti-family and reason for a boycott.
[111] Gayle White, "Southern Baptists vs. Disney; Is the Boycott Working?," The Atlanta Journal and Constitution, 7 March 1998, O1; Deborah Kovach Caldwell, "Dissin' Disney: Boycott Effort Intensifies," News & Record, 28 December 1997, D2; Deborah Kovach Caldwell, "Disney Under Fire Again," The News and Observer, 7 November 1997, E1; "Groups Join Baptist Boycott of Disney," The Advocate, 13 July 1996, 1E; and Marla Dickerson, "Christian Group Escalates Boycott Against Disney," Los Angeles Times, 2 July 1996, D1.
[112] "Family Group Attacks Disney Music," The Washington Times, 3 July 1997, B7.
[113] "A Kick in the Pants," Star Tribune, 20 May 1992, 2D and "Wildmon Calls for Boycott of Levi's Because Levi's in Boycotting Scouts," The Atlanta Journal-Constitution, 19 May 1992, A3.

The American Family Association has been active in governmental issues as well. The group has actively opposed the National Endowment for the Arts.[114] AFA has also been involved in various textbook controversies around the country.[115] It has raised opposition to things like the nomination of Jocelyn Elders as Surgeon General[116] and laws that would legalize same-sex marriages.[117]

AFA opened a Washington office in 1993 to "ensure that the concerns of the growing numbers of AFA supporters are known to Congress, the White house, and agency decision makers."[118] The office was closed a few years later.

Finally, an example of AFA's attempts at influencing legislation is instructive. Representative Bill Hughes (D-NJ) sponsored a child pornography bill.[119] AFA announced that the bill was languishing in committee and told its supporters to call Rep. Hughes.[120] The calls came in at a rate of a thousand a day for five weeks and took all of the office staff's time.[121] The calls were both of support and from people who angrily thought that Hughes was holding up the bill.[122] The torrents of calls so immobilized the office that the staff had no time to actually work on the bill, and, thus, it was delayed for weeks.[123] This example

---

[114] Muriel Dobbin, "Unrelenting Foes Push to Eliminate Arts Agency," Sacramento Bee, 29 June 1997, A1; Kim Masters, "Arts Agency Chairman Defends Film Grant; 'Poison' Not Obscene, NEA's Frohnmayer Says," The Washington Post, 30 March 1991, C1; Bruce Selcraig, "America's Art Critic," St. Petersburg Times, 6 October 1990, 4E; and Bruce Selcraig, "Reverend Wildmon's War of the Arts," The New York Times, 2 September 1990, 22.

[115] Robert O'Harrow, "Fairfax School Board Rejects Appeal for Textbook Disclaimer; Parents Found Creationism Reference Demeaning," The Washington Post, 30 May 1997, D6 and "Rally Planned to Protest Health Textbooks' Approval," Austin American-Statesman, 5 January 1994, B3.

[116] Joyce Price, "Conservative Coalition Targets Nominee for Surgeon General," The Washington Times, 27 June 1993, A1.

[117] "Protecting Traditional Marriage," The Indianapolis Star, 14 June 1996, D2.

[118] Brooks Boliek, "Mr. Wildmon Goes to Washington; Longtime Critic of Hollywood Opens Capital Office, Preps Radio Show," The Hollywood Reporter, 21 April 1993,

[119] William E. Gibson, "Preacher's Campaign for Anti-porn Law Slows Effort to Pass It; Phone Calls, Letters Swamp Bill's Sponsor," The Orange County Register, 26 June 1988, A21.

[120] Gibson, A21.

[121] Gibson, A21.

[122] Gibson, A21.

[123] Gibson, A21.

demonstrates the power of the AFA along with a certain naiveté of the governmental process.

Broadcast Indecency

While Donald Wildmon and the American Family Association have been active since 1977, AFA did not become involved in the FCC's regulation of broadcast indecency until the late 1980s. Some of the earliest efforts by AFA came in the form of letter-writing campaigns to encourage the FCC to enforce the statutory ban on indecency.[124] In addition, according to the FCC, one of the complaints that sparked the FCC's April 1987 letter to Howard Stern came from Wildmon himself.[125]

In fact, the American Family Association has been, in the words of one reporter "spoiling to teach Howard Stern a lesson."[126] AFA has been in the vanguard of the anti-Stern sentiment over the last decade.[127] The group petitioned the FCC in 1995 to refuse to allow Infinity Broadcasting to acquire more stations.[128] That request was rejected by the Commission.[129]

The Michigan chapter of the American Family Association is leading AFA's pursuit of Stern. It maintains the "Howard Stern Information & [sic]

---

[124] Paul Farhi, "War of the Words," The Washington Post, 21 May 1995, W12. and Alex S. Jones, "FCC Studies 'Indecency' on Radio," The New York Times, 22 November 1986, 9.
[125] Allan Parachini and Dennis McDougal, "Art in the Eighties; Censorship: A Decade of Tighter Control of the Arts," Los Angeles Times, 25 December 1989, F1; Dennis McDougal, "FCC Won't Back Off From April Indecency Ruling; More Explicit Programming After Midnight," Los Angeles Times, 25 November 1987, 6-1; Dennis McDougal, "FCC Versus Howard Stern: Agency's 'Indecency' Ruling Hasn't Stopped N.Y. Deejay," Los Angeles Times, 19 August 1987, 6-1; Susan Heller Anderson, "Stern's Station Rebuts FCC Charges," The New York Times, 22 December 1986, C16; and "Racy DJ Gets WXRK in Trouble," The Record, 18 November 1986, A1.
[126] Farhi, "War of the Words," W12.
[127] Dennis McDougal, "At Issue: 'Indecency' Still Murky Issue," Los Angeles Times, 19 February 1988, Part 6-1.
[128] Farhi, "War of the Words," W12.
[129] Farhi, "War of the Words," W12.

Action Page" on AFA's web server, which provides Stern news updates, and lists of the stations that broadcast Stern, as well as the companies that advertise on those stations.[130] The page also requests volunteers to monitor Stern's program.[131] According to the page, Howard Stern's program encourages people, particularly the young, to seek "gratification in inappropriate ways" that eventually leads to "abortion, drugs, theft, murder, and a wide variety of other forms of mayhem directed at others and ultimately contributes to the further breakdown and destruction of the American culture."[132] In response, Howard Stern refers to Donald Wildmon as the "Tupelo Ayatollah."[133]

Despite the AFA-organized, anti-Stern letter-writing campaigns that have bombarded the FCC over the years, most of the fines issued against Stern resulted from complaints filed by another source, Las Vegas resident Al Westcott.[134] Nonetheless, an AFA member has claimed responsibility for one of the indecency fines handed down in 1988. The complaint in the first post-1987 April fine against television station KZKC was authored by an officer in the Kansas City chapter of AFA.[135]

The American Family Association has been active for more than twenty years in trying to clean up the media. Its main weapon has been the economic boycott. As this section has shown, the results have been mixed. AFA's forays into the regulation of indecency have had some success, such as its role in encouraging the FCC to resume enforcement of the indecency policy in 1987. But its efforts since, including trying to keep Infinity Broadcasting from acquiring new licenses, have been largely unsuccessful.

---

130 American Family Association of Michigan. "Howard Stern Information & Action Page." [http://www.afa.net/stern/]. June 1998.
131 AFA of Michigan web site.
132 AFA of Michigan web site.
133 McDougal, "FCC Versus Howard Stern," 6-1.
134 Farhi, "War of the Words," W12

Summary

This chapter presented the history, mission, and goals of Morality in Media and the American Family Association. The purpose of this chapter was to provide further context for the findings and conclusions of this research. The source for this information came from the groups themselves and major media outlets.

Morality in Media has been widely involved in the regulation of indecency, obscenity, and pornography since its founding in 1968. The organization has been active on the federal, state, and local level. MIM's choice of weapon against pornography is the law, working with prosecutors and police in its effort to remove pornography from the public view.

Morality in Media has likened the broadcast of indecent material to public nudity and has worked for more than twenty years to encourage the FCC to enforce the statutory ban on indecent material. The organization is credited with pressuring the FCC into actively enforcing the indecency policy in 1987, after nearly a decade of non-enforcement.

The American Family Association, by contrast, has more often chosen the economic boycott as a means to convince advertisers and program producers to clean up the media. AFA has boycotted companies like Disney and Levi-Strauss, and threatened boycotts of many others. The results of the boycotts have been mixed.

AFA's actions regarding the broadcast of indecent material has also had mixed results. While it has been successful in getting the FCC to issue the April 1987 letter to Infinity, the campaign to deny Infinity Broadcasting new licenses failed.

---

[135] McDougal, "Murky Situation," 6-1.

The material presented in this chapter is an overview of what the groups have done. The next chapter of this research presents the findings of this research, including far more detailed evidence of the groups involvement in the regulation of indecency by the Federal Communications Commission. Six topics are covered, including, among others, the groups' use of the complaint process and nomination hearings to impact the decision-making of the FCC.

Chapter 5
Research Findings:
Evidence of American Family Association and Morality in Media Influence on Indecency Regulation

This chapter presents the findings of the research on the impact of the American Family Association and Morality in Media on the regulation of broadcast indecency. Six areas where AFA and MIM could possibly influence the Federal Communications Commission were examined. Four involved direct contact with the FCC: complaint files, petitions to deny licenses/transfers, lobbying and ex parte presentations, and comments on Notices of Inquiry and Notices of Proposed Rule-Makings. The other two involve the groups' activities via Congress, including involvement in the nomination hearings of FCC Commissioners and oversight hearings.

The following sections describe in depth the material found in each of the areas of influence. Each section provides the facts, analysis occurs in the next chapter.

Complaint Files

There are two kinds of complaints that a member of the public can submit to the FCC regarding the performance of a station. The first is a formal, complete complaint. In the case of indecency, the complaint is considered incomplete if it does not contain the call letters of the station, the time of the broadcast in question, as well as a tape or transcript of the broadcast. Only formal, complete complaints are investigated by the Commission. An investigation involves a Letter of Inquiry being sent to the station, followed by the station's response. If the Commission finds that the broadcast was, in fact, indecent, a Notice of Apparent Liability (a fine) is issued.

The public may also write to the FCC complaining about a station's overall performance in an informal complaint. These complaints do not usually make reference to a specific broadcast or include a transcript. Many of these complaints simply express the individual's disapproval of a station's programming or practices. These complaints are not formally investigated. Rather, they are placed in the station's file for consideration at renewal time.

Previous to the forty-one fines issued between 1989 and 1997, the American Family Association and Morality in Media were involved in the regulation of indecent speech by complaints on three occasions. The complaint regarding the 1973 broadcast of the George Carlin monologue on Pacifica Foundation's station WBAI came from a member of Morality in Media. In fact, the man in question was a minister who was on MIM's national planning board.[1] MIM was also involved in the complaints that led to the Commission's April 1987 letters. Mary Keeley, the Philadelphia woman who submitted one of the two complaints that was cited by the Commission as responsible for the letter issued to Infinity for the broadcast of the "Howard Stern Show,"[2] complained to

---

[1] Morality in Media. "Morality in Media Homepage." [http://pw2.netcom.com/~mimnyc/index.html]. June, 1998 and Lois P. Sheinfeld, "FCC Doublespeak," Film Comment, September/October, 87-90.

[2] In the Matter of Infinity Broadcasting, 2 FCC Rcd 2705 (1987).

the Commission on the advice of MIM.[3] The other complaint discussed by the FCC that sparked the 1987 letter against Stern came from the Reverend Donald Wildmon himself, when the organization was still called the National Federation for Decency.[4]

These three are the most commonly known occasions when AFA and MIM attempted to influence the FCC's regulation of indecency through the complaint process. The complaint files at the FCC headquarters in Washington, D.C., contain other evidence, documented below.

The research into the complaints filed with the FCC looked at twenty-five station files housed at the Complaints and Compliance office in Washington, D.C., and the National Records Center in Suitland, MD.[5] The stations were chosen because they had been fined for violations of the indecency regulations in the years between 1989 and 1997. Most of the files contained little, some included only the formal complaint that had resulted in the fine and the notice that the fine had been paid. Most of those fines resulted from formal complaints submitted by people who did not openly identify themselves with either the American Family Association or Morality in Media.

The largest complaint files, by far, at the Commission were the stations that broadcast the Howard Stern Show, particularly WXRK-FM in New York and WYSP-FM in Philadelphia. The FCC filed most of the generic Stern complaints in

---

[3] MIM web site.

[4] 2 FCC Rcd 2705.

[5] The records at the National Record Center in Suitland, MD were examined to see how far back the organized campaigns went. The author found no evidence of any organized letter-writing campaigns in those files. It appears that most of the effort against Stern came in 1993 and 1994, the same time that the largest fines were being issued. The author looked at the following files: WXRK, 1986 through 1993 (Accession No. 173-95-50, Box 4, National Record Center, Suitland, MD); WYSP, 1986 through 1993 (Accession No. 173-95-50, Box 3, National Record Center, Suitland, MD); and WWDC-FM, Stern's employer from 1981 to 1985 (Accession No. 173-84-31, Box 61 and Accession No. 173-95-50, Box 1, National Record Center, Suitland, MD).

the WXRK file, the originating station of the Howard Stern Show.[6] The WXRK file alone contained thousands of letters, creating a stack more than three feet high. Most of the letters in those files were informal complaints, protesting the nature of Stern's program.[7]

With the exception of one group of pre-printed postcards, most of the letters in the WXRK and WYSP files appear to be spontaneous, individual complaints. Upon further examination, however, the letters show evidence of organized campaigns. For example, many letters sent in early 1994, including dozens of pre-printed cards from listeners in New Jersey,[8] were addressed to Commissioner James *Quillo* -- a misspelling of Commissioner James Quello's name.[9] This misspelling appeared in a 1994 issue of the AFA Journal, in an article that asked that people write to the Commission regarding indecency.[10] The appearance of this misspelling in the AFA Journal shortly before the FCC was inundated with letters including this misspelling is likely not a coincidence. Rather, it appears to be the result of an AFA call to action.

Another point that lends to the idea of organized campaigns is that many of the letters in the WXRK file came from listeners in areas where Howard Stern is not broadcast. Some of these letters openly say that they have never heard Stern on the radio and have only read about his show or have been told to

---

[6] All of the letters mentioned below can be found in the files of the FCC Complaints and Compliance Office in Washington, D.C. Almost all of the letters referenced are in the WXRK-FM file. Similar letters appear in the WYSP-FM file.
[7] Examples of the letters mentioned in this section are available from the author.
[8] See, for example, the postcard from Mrs. Wendy T Cawley, received at the Commission on March 28, 1994. This card and others like it can be found in the WXRK file in the FCC's Complaints and Compliance Office, Washington, D.C.
[9] See, for example, the letter from Mr. Joe McKean, received at the Commission on February 8, 1994. This letter and others like it can be found in the WXRK file in the FCC's Complaints and Compliance Office, Washington, D.C.
[10] AFA Journal, January 1994.

complain.[11] Some of these letters include the Quillo misspelling as well. This suggests that people receive publications like the AFA Journal and respond to the many articles published there about Howard Stern.

Other commonalties among many of the letters also give evidence of organized campaigns. One example is that while they contain misspellings and grammatical mistakes that suggest a lower level of education, the letters exhibit a sophisticated knowledge of the legal issues surrounding the regulation of indecency. Many of the letters quote statistics from the 1990 FCC Report on broadcast indecency.[12] The letters show knowledge of topics like the exact hours of the safe harbor,[13] Senator's Helms' support of the 24-hour ban,[14] and the amounts and numbers of fines issued.[15] While this information was published in the popular press, some matters that were not widely published also appeared in many letters. For example, many people wrote about specific matters that were raised in the Notices of Apparent Liability sent to the stations[16] and others knew exactly when Infinity's stations were up for renewal.[17] Commonalties among these hundreds of letters, including the dates on which they were sent, make it

---

[11] See, for example, the letter from Mr. and Mrs. Tim Dalbey, received at the Commission on January 11, 1994. This letter and others like it can be found in the WXRK file in the FCC's Complaints and Compliance Office, Washington, D.C.

[12] See, for example, the letter from Ms. Becky Ahrens, received at the Commission on June 4, 1993. This letter and others like it can be found in the WXRK file in the FCC's Complaints and Compliance Office, Washington, D.C.

[13] See, for example, the letter from Mrs. Gayle Small, received at the Commission on January 22, 1994. This letter and others like it can be found in the WXRK file in the FCC's Complaints and Compliance Office, Washington, D.C.

[14] Examples of this can be found in the WXRK file in the FCC's Complaints and Compliance Office, Washington, D.C.

[15] See, for example, the letter from Mr. Dwight Smith, received at the Commission on June11, 1993. This letter and others like it can be found in the WXRK file in the FCC's Complaints and Compliance Office, Washington, D.C.

[16] See, for example, the letter from Mr. and Mrs. Clyde Buehler, received at the Commission on January 24, 1994. This letter and others like it can be found in the WXRK file in the FCC's Complaints and Compliance Office, Washington, D.C.

[17] See, for example, the letter from Ms. Joanne Rice. This letter and others like it can be found in the WXRK file in the FCC's Complaints and Compliance Office, Washington, D.C.

unlikely that the letter writers were responding to newspaper reports of the events or writing independently.

A final commonality that lends to the interpretation that most of these hundreds of letters were the product of an organized writing campaign is the use of common phrasings. In early 1993, many letters expressed the wish that the FCC "restrict expansion or license renewals to those broadcasters guilty of violations."[18] The chance that all the letter writers chose that exact phrase independently is unlikely. Along those same lines, many of the letters sent in 1994 urge the FCC to take "quick and decisive action against all pending complaints."[19] A final example of the commonality of phrasing is that many letters sent in 1993 ask the FCC to "move" Howard Stern to the safe harbor.[20] While the FCC does not have such power over programming, the request was included in dozens of letters.

Many of these commonalties can be tied to the American Family Association through the AFA Journal. The Quillo misspelling appeared in the publication.[21] In addition, the Quillo misspelling appeared on many of the letters than included the "quick and decisive" quote, thus tying those letters to AFA.[22] A handful of the letters mentioned that they were complaining in response to a request from AFA and those letters often contained the things mentioned above

---

[18] See, for example, the letter from Mr. and Mrs. Buzzy Keith, received at the Commission on March 29, 1993. This letter and others like it can be found in the WXRK file in the FCC's Complaints and Compliance Office, Washington, D.C.
[19] See, for example, the letter from Ms. Jeanine Heller, received at the Commission on January 13, 1994. This letter and others like it can be found in the WXRK file in the FCC's Complaints and Compliance Office, Washington, D.C.
[20] See, for example, the letter from Ms. Adrienne Ballow, received at the Commission on May 24, 1993. This letter and others like it can be found in the WXRK file in the FCC's Complaints and Compliance Office, Washington, D.C.
[21] AFA Journal, January 1994.
[22] See, for example, the letter from Ms. Jeanine Heller, received at the Commission on January 13, 1994. This letter and others like it can be found in the WXRK file in the FCC's Complaints and Compliance Office, Washington, D.C.

like the "pending complaints" quote.[23] A few complaints even included a page ripped from the AFA Journal with the letters.[24]

It is apparent from the evidence presented above that the American Family Association has been very successful in mobilizing its members to write to the FCC. Morality in Media, on the other hand, appears to have less of a presence in the complaint files, either as MIM itself, or as the instigator of letter-writing campaigns. Aside from the two occasions mentioned earlier in this chapter, MIM appears in the complaint files only twice. One person who wrote a letter complaining about Stern mentions in passing that she is a member of Morality in Media.[25] The only other MIM connection that the author was able to find appeared in the file of New Orleans station WEZB-FM.[26] One of the letters included in that file attached a form letter sent to "Concerned Members of the Business Community" from MIM discussing a program called "Love Phones." The letter encouraged people to contact the sponsors of the program, asking them to drop the program as well as writing to the FCC. [27] A few of the letters in the WEZB file appear to be connected to that mass mailing,[28] but nothing on the scope of the response to the AFA calls to action.

It appears that AFA has been far more active in the use of the complaint process than MIM. Evidence presented here leads to the conclusion that AFA has urged many of its members to write in support of greater enforcement of the

---

[23] Examples of this can be found in the WXRK file in the FCC's Complaints and Compliance Office, Washington, D.C.

[24] Examples of this can be found in the WXRK file in the FCC's Complaints and Compliance Office, Washington, D.C.

[25] The name on this letter was unreadable. It was dated March 15, 1991. It can be found in the WXRK file in the FCC's Complaints and Compliance Office, Washington, D.C.

[26] The file can be found in the FCC's Complaints and Compliance Office, Washington, D.C.

[27] Letter from Mr. and Mrs. Benfield, received at the Commission on July 12, 1995. This letter can be found in the WEZB file in the FCC's Complaints and Compliance Office, Washington, D.C.

indecency regulation. But, complaints are not the only way that citizen groups can affect the FCC's actions. Another method is to protest the renewal of a station's license or the company's acquisition of new licenses. The attempts of the groups to impact the process in this manner are discussed in the next section.

Blocking Renewals and Acquisitions

According to a search of the FCC Record, there have been three occasions when the FCC has responded to an American Family Association or Morality in Media request to block the renewal of a station's license or the acquisition of a new license by the station's parent company because of the broadcast of indecent material. The petitions themselves were not examined.[29] This section relies on the statements made by the FCC in granting the renewals or new licenses. The first example of this course of action came shortly after the 1978 Pacifica decision and was previously described in Chapter 3.

In 1978, Morality in Media petitioned the Commission to deny renewal of the license of WGBH-TV on the grounds that the station had broadcast material that was "offensive," "vulgar," and "harmful to children."[30] Citing programs like "Masterpiece Theatre" and "Monty Python's Flying Circus," the group claimed that under federal and state law the Commission should not allow WGBH to continue broadcasting under the current management. In the order that renewed the station's license, the Commission stated that it had "no general prerogative to intervene in any case where words similar or identical to those in Pacifica are

---

[28] Examples of letters include Mr. Greg Durel, received at the Commission in July, 1995. This letter and others like it can be found in the WEZB file in the FCC's Complaints and Compliance Office, Washington, D.C.

[29] The reports of the Commission on the its decision to allow the transfers contained all the information necessary.

[30] 69 FCC.2d 1250 (1978).

broadcast over a licensed radio or television station."[31] The FCC approved the license renewal on the grounds that the WGBH situation was not the "verbal shock treatment" at issue in Pacifica.[32]

The WGBH challenge appears to be the only time that Morality in Media tried to block a station's license renewal. According to the FCC Record, the American Family Association tried to block Infinity Broadcasting's attempts to acquire additional stations on two occasions.

In 1992, the American Family Association, among others, sent an informal objection to the FCC on the matter of Infinity's intended purchase of three stations licensed to the Cook-Inlet group.[33] AFA claimed that granting the applications for the three additional stations would give Infinity the opportunity to spread Howard Stern into Atlanta, Boston, and Chicago.[34] AFA stated that this would be contrary to the public interest because of Stern's violations of the indecency regulations.[35]

The Commission stated that enforcement proceedings were the "proper forum in which to resolve the allegations of indecent programming,"[36] and cited the $600,000 fine that had been issued to Infinity that same day as sufficient punishment.[37] Concurrences by Commissioners James Quello and Andrew Barrett pointed out that not approving the transfer would punish Cook-Inlet for Infinity's wrong-doings. Thus, the FCC denied AFA's objections and approved the transfer.

---

[31] 69 FCC.2d 1250, 1254.
[32] 69 FCC.2d 1250, 1254.
[33] 8 FCC Rcd 2714 (1992).
[34] 8 FCC Rcd 2714, 2714.
[35] 8 FCC Rcd 2714, 2714.
[36] 8 FCC Rcd 2714, 2714.
[37] 8 FCC Rcd 2688 (1992).

AFA tried once again in 1993 to block an Infinity purchase.[38] Infinity had announced its intentions to buy KRTH-FM, Los Angeles. AFA filed an informal objection to the purchase, again citing the pattern of indecent broadcasts by Howard Stern. Despite the fact that another set of fines had been issued in the years between the Cook-Inlet purchase and KRTH deal, and still another set were issued on the same day as the transfer application was approved,[39] the Commission determined that the pattern of indecent broadcasts did not disqualify Infinity as a licensee.[40]

These three instances show that the FCC has consistently denied citizen groups' petitions to find a licensee unfit because of indecent broadcasts. The next section examines the effect of informal communication between citizen groups and the Commission regarding the regulation of indecent speech.

Lobbying and Ex Parte Communication

As detailed in the research by Crigler and Byrnes,[41] the time immediately before the issuance of the April 1987 letters was fraught with personal communications between the anti-indecency citizen groups and the Federal Communications Commission. Before 1985, there appears to be little evidence of any lobbying. That changed in 1986 and 1987, when a high level of contact between the groups and the Commission is apparent. This section details informal communications between the Commission and MIM and AFA, including the picketing activities of the groups; the coordination between the FCC and the groups in the selection of test cases; and the interpersonal contact that took place

---

[38] 9 FCC Rcd 7112 (1994).
[39] 9 FCC Rcd 1746 (1994).
[40] 9 FCC Rcd 7112, 7114.
[41] John Crigler and William J. Byrnes, "Decency Redux: The Curious History of the New FCC Broadcast Indecency Policy," Catholic University Law Review 38:Winter (1989): 329-363.

between the Commission staff and the groups, including letters, phone calls, and meetings.[42]

The hallmark of Mark Fowler's tenure at the Commission was deregulation in all aspects.[43] Fowler, who once described television as "a toaster with pictures," thought that the market should take care of the quality of the content on the broadcast media.[44] During his tenure, complaints poured into the Commission regarding the prevalence of sexually explicit material on radio and television.[45] Despite the volume of complaints, he did not take any action.

In the summer of 1986, as the time for Fowler's re-nomination approached, Morality in Media began picketing the FCC headquarters in Washington.[46] MIM and other anti-indecency groups opposed Fowler on the grounds that he had "failed completely to uphold decency standards on radio and television."[47] The groups also organized a letter-writing campaign to the Senate Commerce Committee opposing Fowler.[48] In addition, Reverend Wildmon sent a letter in October to Senator John Danforth, requesting that he be allowed to testify at Fowler's re-nomination hearing.[49]

When Ronald Reagan announced that Dennis Patrick would take Fowler's place as FCC Chair, the picketing began anew. Members of the National Decency Forum, a coalition group which included both MIM and AFA, demonstrated in

---

[42] A narrative of this time is presented in the Crigler and Byrnes article.
[43] Mark S. Fowler and Daniel L. Brenner, "A Marketplace Approach to Broadcast Regulation," Texas Law Review 60 (1982): 207.
[44] Fowler and Brenner, 207.
[45] "Its Official; Patrick for FCC Chairmanship," Broadcasting, 9 February 1987, 43.
[46] Crigler and Byrnes, 344.
[47] Henry Klingeman, "Fowler Play, Renomination of FCC Chairman Mark Fowler," National Review, 21 November 1986, 30.
[48] Crigler and Byrnes, 344.
[49] Letter from Donald E. Wildmon, Executive Director, National Federation for Decency, to John C. Danforth, Senator, United States Senate (September 9, 1986). This letter was part of a FOIA request made by John Crigler as research for his 1989 article, Decency Redux: The Curious History of the New FCC Broadcast Indecency Policy. A copy of the entire FOIA record is on file with the author.

front of the FCC.[50] The group was demonstrating in support of a nomination for Jack Smith, the former General Counsel of the Commission. Smith was the driving force behind the April 1987 letters that expanded the scope of indecency regulation and had made a pledge to the group to actively oppose indecency.[51] The group even went to the White House, asking Pat Buchannan, Reagan's Director of Communications, to ask for the withdrawal of Patrick's name in favor of Smith's.[52]

Picketing was just one way that the groups lobbied the Commission for changes in the indecency policy. The groups also had face-to-face meetings and exchanged letters with members of the staff and Chairman Fowler himself. One of a series of exchanges between the citizen groups and the Commission involved selecting the broadcasts that would provide the test cases for an expanded enforcement of the indecency regulations. For example, according to Crigler and Byrnes, MIM's advice to Mary Keeley about complaining to the Commission regarding Howard Stern came directly from Jack Smith, the FCC general counsel.[53] That complaint was one of the two that resulted in the April 1987 letter to Infinity Broadcasting.

Another example of the groups involvement in the selection of test cases can be seen in letters exchanged between Reverend Wildmon and Jack Smith. In one letter, dated August 25, 1986, Wildmon sent Smith a tape of a broadcast of the movie, The Rose, which had been shown unedited on a Memphis television station.[54] Smith later replied "as we discussed on the phone today, I do not

---

[50] "It's Official," 43.
[51] Leonard Zeidenberg, "Indecency: Radio's Sound, FCC's Fury," Broadcasting, 22 June 1987, 46.
[52] "It's Official," 43.
[53] Crigler and Byrnes, 345.
[54] Letter from Donald E. Wildmon, Executive Director, National Federation for Decency to John B. Smith, General Counsel, Federal Communications Commission (August 25, 1986), Crigler FOIA request. On file with the author.

believe this presents the kind of air-tight case that you want to push at this time."[55] He went on to say that the Commission was considering a few other cases that "may be more clear violations."[56] On another occasion, Reverend Wildmon sent a tape and transcript of a Chicago talk show, encouraging the Commission to take action for this violation of the indecency policy.[57]

Letters, memoranda, and appointment calendars show that Jack Smith and Mark Fowler met with members of anti-indecency groups a number of times in 1986.[58] In fact, after one such meeting, Brad Curl, head of the National Decency Forum, promised to cancel the protests on the basis of the understanding reached during these meetings that the FCC would step up its enforcement activity.[59]

This section has shown that FCC staff and Commissioners interacted with anti-indecency groups prior to the announcement of the April 1987 decisions. Some, including Erwin Krasnow, have speculated that the April letters represented an attempt to "placate" those groups.[60] While the protests in front of the Commission stopped not long after the April letters, the letter writing

---

[55] Letter from John B. Smith, General Counsel, Federal Communications Commission to Donald E. Wildmon, Executive Director, National Federation for Decency (September 19, 1986), Crigler FOIA request. On file with the author.
[56] Letter from John B. Smith, General Counsel, Federal Communications Commission to Donald E. Wildmon, Executive Director, National Federation for Decency (September 19, 1986) , Crigler FOIA request. On file with the author.
[57] Letter from Donald E. Wildmon, Executive Director, National Federation for Decency to John B. Smith, General Counsel, Federal Communications Commission (November 18, 1986) , Crigler FOIA request. On file with the author.
[58] Letter from Paul McGeady, General Counsel, Morality in Media to John B. Smith, General Counsel, Federal Communications Commission (July 23, 1986); Letter from Brad Curl, National Director, Morality in Media to Mark Fowler, Chairman, Federal Communications Commission (February 23, 1987); Letter from Brad Curl, Chairman, National Decency Forum to Mark Fowler, Chairman, Federal Communications Commission (June 30, 1986); Appointment calendar for Mark Fowler, Chairman, Federal Communication Commission, four p.m. meeting with Brad Curl (July 2, 1986); and Federal Communications Commission Memorandum, from Jack Smith, General Counsel, Federal Communications Commission, to Mark Fowler, Chairman, Federal Communications Commission, describing a meeting between Brad Curl, National Federation for Decency, and Smith (July 21, 1986). Crigler FOIA request. On file with the author.
[59] Crigler and Byrnes, 345.
[60] Erwin G. Krasnow, "The Politics of Program Regulation," Broadcasting, 2 November 1987, 28.

campaigns to the Commission continued. The groups also used formal channels of participation at the Commission, such as Notices of Inquiry and Notices of Proposed Rulemaking to further their cause.[61]

Notices of Inquiry and Notices of Proposed Rulemaking

The Federal Communications Commission has several procedures in place for gathering public comment on an impending action or rule. Two of these are the Notice of Inquiry (NOI) and the Notice of Proposed Rulemaking (NPRM).[62] An NOI typically describes a problem and asks for public comment on how to solve it.[63] An NPRM, on the other hand, is when the Commission outlines a specific change to its rules and asks for public comment on the proposal.[64] The Commission has twice used these methods of gathering public comment in regards to the regulation of indecency: an NOI in 1989 and an NPRM in 1992.

NOIs and NPRMs provide an excellent opportunity for citizen groups to comment on the processes of the Commission. Morality in Media filed comments in both the NOI and NPRM. The American Family Association commented only on the NOI. This section compares the comments filed by the groups with the final reports of the Commission on these actions. That comparison may yield evidence of citizen group influence on the FCC.

[61] The FCC Record shows that Morality in Media made ex parte presentations to the Commission on two occasions in the 1990s. Nothing beyond the fact that there was contact and the topic was broadcast indecency is present in the Record.
[62] Robert L. Hilliard, The Federal Communications Commission: A Primer (Stoneham, MA: Butterworth-Heimnemann, 1991), 115.
[63] Hilliard, 72.
[64] Hilliard, 72.

NOI on Broadcast Indecency, Docket 89-494

In 1989, the FCC issued an NOI on the topic of the 24-hour ban on indecency. This was done in order to build a record on the necessity of the ban, as ordered by the D.C. Court of Appeals in ACT II.[65] The NOI listed several areas in which the Commission wished to establish a record, including the definition of children, information on children's media usage, and alternatives to the ban. The response to the NOI was overwhelming. In addition to the eighteen formal comments and fourteen reply comments, the FCC received 92,500 informal comments from the public.[66] The Commission report states that 88,000 of the comments were in favor of the ban and 4,500 were against it.[67] Due to the fact that most of those informal comments have disappeared from the Commission's files,[68] as was discussed in Chapter 1, this section focuses on the formal comments and reply comments filed by MIM and AFA.

Morality in Media's comments and reply comments,[69] which were heavily laced with quotations from a wide variety of court decisions, focused on three main areas. The first was that the protection of children should not be the sole rationale for the regulation of indecency.[70] The group spent seventeen pages detailing why the scope of the regulation should not, under legal precedent, be limited to children. Among other concerns, the group maintained that the adult's right to privacy in the home was a strong justification for the ban.[71] MIM also

---

[65] In the Matter of Enforcement of Prohibitions Against Broadcast Indecency in 18 U.S.C. § 1464, 4 FCC Rcd 8358 (1989).
[66] In the Matter of Enforcement of Prohibitions Against Broadcast Indecency in 18 U.S.C. § 1464, 5 FCC Rcd 5297 (1990).
[67] 5 FCC Rcd 5297, 5297.
[68] Only a handful of the informal comments are in the docket file in the FCC Reference Room. No one at the Commission seems to know where the material has gone.
[69] After the comments are received by the Commission, the public is allowed to read them and submit a rebuttal to anything stated in the comments. These are known as reply comments.
[70] Comments of Morality in Media, Docket #89-494, 2-18.
[71] Comments of Morality in Media, Docket #89-494, 12.

claimed that indecency should be regulated as a "public nuisance,"[72] and that Congress had the authority to prohibit indecent material on the basis that it had a duty to keep the channels of commerce free of that "which harms the public morals."[73] This point, that the regulation should reach beyond children to protect all people from the harms of indecency, was the main focus of the MIM comments.

The second point of the group's comments declared that the Supreme Court's decision in Pacifica did not require the FCC to create a safe harbor.[74] MIM wrote that the home should not become "an after-hours hangout for the broadcast pig."[75] The group stated that the public's right to be free of indecent material in the home does not end when the children are asleep.[76] This argument relies heavily on MIM's first point, that more than just children need to be protected from indecent broadcasts.

MIM's final point was that the constitutional test against which the FCC measured indecency regulation was incorrect.[77] This section of the comments addressed the core First Amendment issue of whether indecent broadcast speech is protected speech. The group argued that Pacifica did not require that the regulation be the most narrowly tailored means of advancing a compelling government interest.[78] This constitutional test, supported by the FCC, required that the scope of the regulation be so precise as to not unduly infringe on the rights of others while still serving the compelling government interest in the protection of children. MIM maintained that this position was incorrect. It

---

[72] Comments of Morality in Media, Docket #89-494, 7.
[73] Comments of Morality in Media, Docket #89-494, 5.
[74] Comments of Morality in Media, Docket #89-494, 19-23.
[75] Comments of Morality in Media, Docket #89-494, 19. The "broadcast pig" phrase refers to the long-standing analogy used by the courts that a nuisance is like a pig in the parlor, instead of the barnyard.
[76] Comments of Morality in Media, Docket #89-494, 23.
[77] Comments of Morality in Media, Docket #89-494, 23-37.

claimed that the constitutional test should be less strict. Thus, MIM stated that because of the pervasiveness of broadcasting and the distasteful nature of the subject matter at issue, indecency regulation should be treated as "time, place, manner" or "permissible subject matter regulation."[79] This approach would allow stricter regulation of indecency. Thus, restrictions that would fail the compelling interest/narrowly tailored test, would pass constitutional muster under the lower standard. MIM felt that indecency was a nuisance, rather than speech needing protection, and should be regulated as such.

The American Family Association tailored its comments more closely to the NOI than MIM. The comments covered a wide range of topics, and mixed legal quotations with a significant amount of statistical information and analysis. AFA considered many of the questions proposed in the NOI and provided the Commission with the data it requested. AFA wrote that the FCC had been correct in determining that seventeen and under was the appropriate definition of children.[80] This conclusion was based on a compilation of obscenity laws from across the country, illustrating how the states defined a child.[81] AFA also addressed the issue of the presence of children in the broadcast audience as well as the pervasiveness and accessibility of radios and televisions to those children.[82] To support the conclusion that children have complete access to the media at all times and are using the media at all times, AFA relied on a wide variety of sources, including social science and medical research,[83] Nielsen ratings data,[84] and statistics compiled by the government.[85] This section of the comments concluded

---

[78] Comments of Morality in Media, Docket #89-494, 24.
[79] Comments of Morality in Media, Docket #89-494, 32.
[80] Comments of the American Family Association, Docket #89-494, 13.
[81] Comments of the American Family Association, Docket #89-494, 13.
[82] Comments of the American Family Association, Docket #89-494, 13-28.
[83] Comments of the American Family Association, Docket #89-494, 14.
[84] Comments of the American Family Association, Docket #89-494, 16, 24-28.
[85] Comments of the American Family Association, Docket #89-494, 17.

that children are always in the broadcast audience, thus making channeling an ineffective means of protecting them from indecency.

AFA used similar data sources to comment on other questions presented by the Commission. The group used court decisions such as Pacifica and a wide range of social science research to prove the existence of harm to children from indecency.[86] AFA also addressed the issues of parental supervision of children's media usage[87] and the effectiveness of ratings and warnings in aiding that supervision.[88] The group found that supervision was difficult, if not impossible, and ratings and warnings were ineffective. Again, AFA relied on governmentally gathered statistics[89] and social science literature to reach this conclusion.

In order to prove that children have access to VCRs and use them to time shift programming, AFA presented statistics on the number of children who use VCRs. These statistics were from studies done by the government, the media, and the academic community.[90] Similar research was used to support the ineffectiveness of technological alternatives to the 24-hour ban[91] and the availability of non-broadcast sources of indecent material.[92]

The final report of the Commission, issued in 1990, found that the 24-hour ban was the most narrowly tailored method of achieving the governmental interest in the protection of children.[93] The Commission concluded that (1) the definition of children should be seventeen and under; (2) children were always in the broadcast audience; (3) channeling, warnings, and blocking technologies were

---

[86] Comments of the American Family Association, Docket #89-494, 11-13 and Reply Comments of the American Family Association, Docket #89-494, 11-31.
[87] Comments of the American Family Association, Docket #89-494, 35-42.
[88] Comments of the American Family Association, Docket #89-494, 42-48.
[89] AFA used sources such as the Statistical Abstract of the United States 1988, prepared by the Bureau of the Census.
[90] Comments of the American Family Association, Docket #89-494, 28-35.
[91] Comments of the American Family Association, Docket #89-494, 48-49.
[92] Comments of the American Family Association, Docket #89-494, 49-52.
[93] 5 FCC Rcd 5297, 5298.

ineffective; and (4) indecent material was available to adults on other media.[94] In reaching this decision, the FCC relied heavily on information provided by MIM and AFA. The rest of this section discusses the points made by the Commission and how they match up with the comments submitted by the groups.

The early part of the report rejected many of the arguments made by the groups in their comments. The first point made by the Report rejected MIM's position that the constitutional test used to measure indecency was incorrect.[95] The FCC held that the compelling interest/narrowly tailored test is required by the Supreme Court's decisions in the area of the regulation of indecency.[96] The FCC also opposed MIM's position that indecency should not be a child-centered regulation. While MIM presented a host of other justifications for the regulation, the Commission maintained that the protection of children was the prevailing rationale for the regulation and refused to expand the scope of the regulation.[97] The Commission also disregarded one of the thrusts of AFA's comments and reply comments: harm. AFA spent many pages presenting material on the issue of the harms children suffer due to being exposed to indecency. The FCC stated that harm was not an issue, and that past court decisions held that the rationale of protecting children was sufficiently strong without actually having to prove any harm.[98]

Although the Commission disagreed with MIM and AFA on the points mentioned above, most of the rest of the FCC Report relied heavily on their comments. On the issue of the pervasiveness of broadcast media, the Commission quoted from both group's comments, AFA's in particular.[99] The Commission

---

[94] 5 FCC Rcd 5297, 5297.
[95] 5 FCC Rcd 5297, 5298.
[96] 5 FCC Rcd 5297, 5298.
[97] 5 FCC Rcd 5297, 5299.
[98] 5 FCC Rcd 5297, 5300.
[99] 5 FCC Rcd 5297, 5302.

presented the ratings data submitted by the groups to prove that children were always in the broadcast audience.[100] The Commission also relied on the statistical and social science data aggregated by the groups to support the stance that children have access to the media at all times.[101] The Report also used the data collected by the groups to support the position that children's exposure to the media was not well supervised.[102] In contrast, the Commission virtually dismissed all statistics provided by the broadcast industry, which held that children were not in the audience at night and thus were not in any danger from indecent broadcasts.[103]

The Commission also based its conclusions about alternatives to the 24-hour ban on the comments of AFA and MIM. The Commission concluded that channeling would be an ineffective means of keeping indecency away from children because they were always in the audience. The FCC relied on the data provided by AFA, rather than the broadcast industry, to reach that conclusion.[104]

In addition, the Commission found that children have access to VCRs which enables them to time shift.[105] The Commission's determination that children use VCRs to time shift programming was based on the AFA comments, as well.[106] The Commission also relied on AFA and MIM in proving that ratings and warnings were ineffective.[107] Finally, the Report also concluded that adults have access to indecency on other media, a conclusion that was supported by quotes from the AFA comment.[108]

---

[100] 5 FCC Rcd 5297, 5203.
[101] 5 FCC Rcd 5297, 5203.
[102] 5 FCC Rcd 5297, 5203.
[103] 5 FCC Rcd 5297, 5203.
[104] 5 FCC Rcd 5297, 5306.
[105] 5 FCC Rcd 5297, 5606.
[106] 5 FCC Rcd 5297, 5306.
[107] 5 FCC Rcd 5297, 5608.
[108] 5 FCC Rcd 5297, 5608.

This section has shown that the 1990 Report of the Commission on the 24-hour ban relied substantially on information submitted by AFA and MIM in response to the NOI.[109] The Commission virtually ignored the information provided by the broadcast industry in favor of that provided by the groups. The next section, examining Docket 92-223, looks to see if the same influence was present again.

NPRM on Broadcast Indecency, Docket 92-223

In October of 1992, the Commission released an NPRM discussing the implementation of the Byrd Amendment. The Amendment required the FCC to prohibit the broadcast of indecent material between midnight and six a.m. The amendment made an exception for public broadcasters who went off the air before midnight, stating that they could broadcast indecent material after ten p.m.[110] The Commission issued the NPRM to supplement the record created with the 1990 Report.

The comments filed on this docket are available on the FCC's Record Imaging Processing System, an electronic database. This docket showed seven entries, one of which came from Morality in Media. The comment was filed late by MIM, due to problems acquiring a copy of the NPRM.[111] Because of this lateness, the comments are very short, containing only the outline of the MIM argument. Essentially, the comments boil down to one point: the decision in Pacifica does not require a safe harbor and thus the Commission should find a way to apply the regulations twenty-four hours a day.

---

[109] Some other groups, including a Mormon licensee, did submit comments, but the bulk of the report relied on the comments from AFA and MIM.

[110] Public Telecommunications Act of 1991, Pub. L. No. 102-356.

[111] Letter from Paul McGeady, General Counsel, Morality in Media, to Donna Searcy, Secretary, Federal Communications Commission (December 12, 1992). Available in the FCC Reference Room, Washington, D.C.

The report of the Commission, issued in January, 1993, incorporates the findings of the 1990 Report.[112] It concludes that nothing had changed since 1990, and the finding that a 24-hour ban was the only means to protect children was still true.[113] However, the Commission wrote that "in light of serious constitutional issues at stake here and the need to balance all interests, we conclude that the channeling approach to broadcast indecency enforcement . . . is reasonable."[114] At no time in the report does the FCC mention the comments filed by Morality in Media.

The previous four sections presented ways in which MIM and AFA could make their positions known to the FCC as well as possibly influencing the decision-making process of the Commission. The next two sections look at the group's attempts to influence the Commission via Congress.

Nomination Hearings

The United States Senate has advise and consent powers over nominations for the five seats on the Federal Communications Commission. Therefore, any person nominated to the FCC by the president must first undergo a hearing in front of the Communications Subcommittee of the Senate Commerce Committee. According to communication scholar Haeryon Kim, the questions asked during the nomination hearings and the witnesses who testify play a significant role in setting the agenda of the Commission.[115]

---

[112] In the Matter of Enforcement of Prohibitions Against Broadcast Indecency in 18 U.S.C. @1464, 8 FCC Rcd 704 (1993).
[113] 8 FCC Rcd 704, 710.
[114] 8 FCC Rcd 704, 710.
[115] Haeryon Kim "Congressional Influence on the FCC: An Analysis of Confirmation hearings for Commission Chairmen, 1969-1989," Communications and the Law 15:4 (1993): 37-54.

Thirty-four hearings held between 1961 and 1994 were examined for the present research.[116] Until 1989, indecency was never an issue at nomination hearings. At most, the senators expressed a general dismay about the levels of sex and violence in the media but focused on other topics. That changed, however, when the confirmation hearings were held for Alfred Sikes, Andrew Barrett, and Sherrie Marshall in July of 1989.[117] That hearing focused almost exclusively on the issue of the regulation of indecent and obscene speech on broadcasting. This came as a surprise to many, including the nominees.[118] After the 1989 hearing, all subsequent FCC nominees were asked about the regulation of indecent speech in their written questionnaires, and most mentioned a dedication to the enforcement

---

[116] The following is a listing of the hearings examined. All hearings were held in front of the Senate Committee on Commerce, Science, and Transportation. Reed E. Hundt, 103rd Cong., 1st. Sess., S. Hrg. 103-349 (1993); Rachelle Chong and Susan Ness, 103rd Cong., 2nd Sess , S. Hrg. 103-55 (1994); James Quello, 102nd Cong., 1st Sess., S. Hrg. 102-306 (1991); Ervin S. Duggan, 101st Cong., 2nd Sess., S. Hrg. 101-573 (1990); Andrew C. Barrett, 101st Cong., 2nd Sess., S. Hrg. 101-726 (1990); Alfred C. Sikes, Sherrie P. Marshall, and Andrew C. Barrett, 101st Cong.,1st. Sess., S. Hrg. 101-256 (1989); Dennis Patrick, 99th Cong., 1st Sess., S. Hrg. 99-344 (1985); Patricia Diaz Dennis, 99th Cong., 2nd Sess., S. Hrg. 99-654 (1986); Dennis Patrick, 98th Cong., 2nd Sess., S. Hrg. 98-740 (1984); James Quello, 98th Cong., 2nd Sess., S. Hrg. 98-983 (1984); Stephen A. Sharp, 97th Cong., 2nd Sess., S. Hrg. 97-131 (1982); Mark Fowler and Mary Dawson, 97th Cong., 1st Sess., S. Hrg. 97-46 (1981); James Quello and Henry M. Rivera, 97th Cong., 1st Sess., S. Hrg. 97-50 (1981); Anne P. Jones, 96th Cong., 1st Sess., S. Hrg. 96-40 (1979); Tyrone Brown, 96th Cong., 1st Sess., S. Hrg. 96-46 (1979); Tyrone Brown, 95th Cong., 1st Sess., S. Hrg. 95-55 (1977); Charles D. Ferris, 95th Cong., 1st Sess., S. Hrg. 95-41 (1977); Joseph R. Fogarty and Margareta White, 94th Cong., 2nd Sess., S. Hrg. 94-103 (1976); Abbott Washburn, 94th Cong., 1st Sess., S. Hrg. 94-39/pt. 3 (1975); James Quello, 93rd Cong., 2nd Sess., S. Hrg. 93-58 (1974); Luther Holcomb, 93rd Cong., 2nd Sess., S. Hrg. 93-83 (1974); Richard E. Wiley, 92nd Cong., 2nd Sess., S. Hrg. 92-55 (1972); Charlotte Reid, 92nd Cong., 1st Sess., S. Hrg. 92-25 (1971); Robert Wells and Thomas Houser, 92nd Cong., 1st Sess., S. Hrg. 92-3 (1971); Dean Burch, 91st Cong., 1st Sess., S1993-3 (1969); H. Rex Lee, 92nd Cong., 2nd Sess., S 1933-1 (1968); Robert E. Lee, 90th Cong., 1st Sess., S1807-4 (1967); Rosel Hyde and Nicholas Johnson, 89th Cong., 2nd Sess., S1783-5 (1966); Robert T. Bartley, 89th Cong., 1st Sess., S1706-8 (1965); James J. Wadsworth, 89th Cong., 1st Sess., S1688-3 (1965); Frederick Ford, 88th Cong., 2nd Sess., S1505-4 (1964); Lee Loevinger, 88th Cong., 1st Sess., S1550-8 (1963); Kenneth Cox, 88th Cong., 1st Sess., S1550-1 (1963); William E. Henry, 87th Cong., 2nd Sess., S1544-1 (1962); and Newton Minow; 87th Cong., 1st Sess., S1433-7 (1961).

[117] Hearings Before the Committee on Commerce, Science, and Transportation, United States Senate, Alfred C. Sikes, Sherrie P. Marshall, and Andrew C. Barrett, To Be Commissioners, Federal Communications Commission, 101st Cong.,1st. Sess., S. Hrg. 101-256, 392 (1989).

[118] Linda Eardley, "More Competition is Goal of Sikes as Head of FCC," St. Louis Post-Dispatch, 8 August 1989, 1B.

of the indecency regulations in their opening remarks.[119] But no hearing ever focused on the regulation of indecency like the Sikes, Barrett, and Marshall hearing. For that reason, as well as the presence of the American Family Association on the witness list, this section focuses exclusively on that 1989 hearing.

The written questionnaires filled out by the nominees prior to the hearing did not mention the issue of indecency. But when the hearing began, the first question asked by Senator Daniel Inuoye was "what do you propose to do about indecency and violence on television?"[120] Sikes responded in an non-committal manner, suggesting that the answer to the question of indecency lies in broadcasters working together to re-establish the NAB code.[121] Barrett said that the committee should recognize that there is a market for the indecent programming.[122] Marshall was the only one of the three to give a clear answer, stating "I am committed to vigorous enforcement of the congressional ban on broadcasting indecent programming."[123]

From there, the hearing ranged over a number of issues, but several senators returned to the topic of indecent programming during their questioning. Senators Albert Gore, Ernest Hollings, and Bob Kasten in particular questioned the nominees closely on their positions on the regulation of indecency. After each question, the nominees more closely aligned themselves with the pro-regulatory position. Towards the end of the hearing, when Senator Kasten asked the

---

[119] Reed E. Hundt, 103rd Cong., 1st. Sess., S. Hrg. 103-349 (1993); Rachelle Chong and Susan Ness, 103rd Cong., 2nd Sess., S. Hrg. 103-55 (1994); James Quello, 102nd Cong., 1st Sess., S. Hrg. 102-306 (1991); Ervin S. Duggan, 101st Cong., 2nd Sess., S. Hrg. 101-573 (1990); Andrew C. Barrett, 101st Cong., 2nd Sess., S. Hrg. 101-726 (1990).
[120] Sikes, Marshall, and Barrett Hearing, 392.
[121] Sikes, Marshall, and Barrett Hearing, 393.
[122] Sikes, Marshall, and Barrett Hearing, 393.
[123] Sikes, Marshall, and Barrett Hearing, 393.

nominees if they would take enforcement action on the matter of broadcast indecency, they all responded with a simple yes.[124]

Following this intense questioning by the subcommittee, a panel of witnesses representing anti-indecency citizen groups appeared. The panel included the Reverend Ray Moore, president of the Palmetto Family Caucus; Peggy Coleman, legal counsel for the American Family Association; and Ed McAteer, president of the Religious Roundtable. Both Moore and McAteer flatly opposed the nomination of Alfred Sikes on the grounds that he had not strongly endorsed the idea of increasing enforcement of indecency. They believed that he would follow in the deregulatory footsteps of Mark Fowler and Dennis Patrick. Peggy Coleman, who was representing both AFA and MIM, took a more general position.

Coleman, who was speaking in the place of an ailing Donald Wildmon, asked the committee to instruct the FCC to enforce the indecency regulations to the fullest extent of the law.[125] A written statement by Donald Wildmon was then placed into the record, which stated that AFA and MIM did not actively oppose the nominees, but rather the inactivity of the Commission.[126] Wildmon went on to say that the groups advocate the suspension and/or revocation of licenses for the broadcast of indecent material.[127] In addition, Wildmon wrote that the members of the Commission should be as "available and responsive to the concerns of the pro-family constituency as they are to those of the broadcast industry."[128]

---

[124] Sikes, Marshall, and Barrett Hearing, 405.
[125] Sikes, Marshall, and Barrett Hearing, 441.
[126] Sikes, Marshall, and Barrett Hearing, 446.
[127] Sikes, Marshall, and Barrett Hearing, 446.
[128] Sikes, Marshall, and Barrett Hearing, 448.

The Committee later approved all three nominees by a vote of 15-2.[129] Senators Gore and John D. Rockefeller, IV cast the dissenting votes as a symbolic gesture against the deregulatory stance of the previous commission.[130] In addition Gore said that the nominees' statements on the regulation of indecency were "inadequate."[131]

Shortly after winning approval of the committee, Sikes told the press that he planned to "act quickly and vigorously to take action against broadcasters who broadcast obscene material" and that since the law governing the regulation of indecency was in flux, the Commission would "carefully analyze what it has the authority to do."[132] All three nominees were later approved by the full Senate.

At the second meeting with Alfred Sikes as chair, the FCC began to take action against licensees for the broadcast of indecent materials by issuing four fines.[133] This occurred only two months after the nomination hearings that focused so heavily on the regulation of indecent speech. As discussed above, the testimony of the American Family Association advocated that the Commission take that action. Thus, on the surface, it appears that the testimony possibly had some influence on the stance of the Commission on the regulation of broadcast indecency. The next section looks at other congressional hearings involving the FCC where citizen groups have played a role.

Oversight Hearings

Congressional hearings offer an excellent opportunity for the public to make its views known to the government. The American Family Association and

---

[129] Linda Eardley, "Nominee for FCC Advances," St. Louis Post-Dispatch, 2 August 1989, 7A.
[130] Eardley, "Nominee," 7A.
[131] Eardley, "Nominee," 7A.
[132] Eardley, "Nominee," 7A.
[133] John Burgess, "FCC Presses 'Indecency' Fight; 4 Radio Stations Fined, Other Sent Letters," The Washington Post, A1.

Morality in Media have used the hearing as a forum to communicate their positions on a number of topics. But there has been only one occasion when the groups have participated in a hearing to make known their positions on the FCC's policy on indecency. That one occasion was the 1989 Sikes, Barrett, and Marshall nomination hearing. Therefore, while the oversight function of Congress may provide an opportunity for citizen groups to make their opinions known, neither MIM or AFA took advantage of it on the matter of broadcast indecency.

Summary

This chapter reviewed the findings of the research designed to find evidence of citizen groups' influence on the Federal Communications Commission. The chapter reviewed six areas where evidence of such impact might be found.

The first area considered was the complaint files at the FCC. Those files, particularly those associated with stations that aired the Howard Stern Show, showed a great deal of evidence of organized letter-writing campaigns.

The second area considered was a number of petitions to deny renewals or transfer licenses filed at the Commission. The research demonstrated that while MIM and AFA have filed such petitions, they have always been unsuccessful.

The third section of this chapter investigated whether the groups had any success with lobbying the Commission's staff. Letters and appointment calendars showed that there was significant lobbying activity during the time before a major shift in the indecency policy occurred.

The fourth area where evidence of the group's impact was examined was the formal comment process. Notices of Inquiry and Proposed Rulemaking relating to the regulation of indecency were examined to see how the comments filed by the groups matched the final reports of the Commission. The evidence showed that while the groups comments were very influential on one report, the comments submitted to a later NOI were ignored.

The fifth and sixth areas of possible influence are related to Congress. Nomination and oversight hearings were examined. The research discovered that the groups only testified once on the matter of the FCC's regulation of broadcast indecency: a 1989 confirmation hearing. That hearing was dominated by calls for increased regulation. Shortly after the nominees were confirmed, the FCC stepped up its regulation of indecency considerably.

The next chapter analyzes the findings discussed here and then place them within the context of the Krasnow, Longley, and Terry model of the Broadcast Policy-Making System.

Chapter 6
Analysis and Conclusions

This chapter presents an analysis of the data discussed in Chapter 5. That chapter examined the six possible avenues of influence: complaint files, petitions to deny licenses, lobbying, Notices of Inquiry and Proposed Rule-Making, nomination and other Congressional hearings, that the American Family Association and Morality in Media may have used to influence the Federal Communications Commission. The ultimate goal of this discussion is to understand how much success the groups had in impacting the policy-making process. The chapter then examines these findings in light of the Krasnow, Longley, and Terry model of the Broadcast Policy-Making System.

Complaint Files

The section on the complaints filed with the Commission can be divided into two parts. The first part includes the early letters that helped spark the test cases which defined the parameters of the regulation of indecency: the George Carlin case and the 1987 letter about the Howard Stern Show. The second part deals with the thousands of letters in the Commission's files about the Howard Stern Show in the 1990s. These two sets of complaints represent the groups' efforts to impact indecency regulation through the complaint process.

The 1973 letter from John Douglas, the minister from Florida who was also on the planning board of Morality in Media, came to the FCC at a time when the Commission was seeking a test case. The agency had already issued small fines to two stations in the hopes that they would seek judicial review.[1] Unlike the earlier stations, Pacifica was willing to appeal and the case eventually went to the U.S. Supreme Court. It is unlikely that MIM foresaw Pacifica's willingness to seek judicial review, and thus the participation of the group in this instance appears to be coincidental.

After nearly a decade of non-enforcement of the indecency policy, the FCC issued the April 1987 letters. The Commission announced in those letters that the definition of indecency would no longer be limited to repetition of the seven words at issue in the Carlin case. One of the three letters went to WYSP-FM, for the broadcast of the Howard Stern Show. Two complaints were responsible for that letter. One came from Reverend Wildmon and the other came from a Philadelphia woman named Mary Keeley. Morality in Media advised Keeley on how to complain to the FCC. The events surrounding these complaints are tied to the intense lobbying effort made by the groups in 1986 and 1987. Thus, analysis of these letters is better suited to the section on lobbying.

The second set of complaints includes the thousands of letters received by the Commission regarding Howard Stern. On the surface, the letters appear to be individual in origin. The research, however, showed that many of these letters were a result of organized campaigns. Commonalties among the letters, like the "Quillo" misspelling, the sophisticated level of legal knowledge, and the many phrases shared among the letters leads to the conclusion that they were solicited. The presence of the name of the American Family Association in some of the letters suggests that the group was behind many of these campaigns.

Once it was determined that AFA was responsible for the thousands of complaints to the Commission, the next step is to ascertain what effect these letters may have had. One area where AFA did not have any impact was in the issuance of fines. The letters from the organized campaigns did not result in any fines. The files of those stations that were fined for a broadcast other than the Howard Stern Show show no obvious evidence of AFA or MIM. In addition, most of the fines against stations airing the Howard Stern Show resulted from complaints sent by one man, Al Westcott, who is not formally associated with any anti-indecency group.[2]

The letters that the FCC received from these organized campaigns were largely general complaints that did not contain the required information to even begin an investigation.[3] According to Thomas Winkler, a staff member in the Complaints and Compliance Office, those complaints that are not "complete" are merely placed in the station's file for consideration at renewal time. Since a station airing Stern's show has never had its license revoked or even had a renewal hearing called for the broadcast of indecent material, this is another area where the groups found little success.

There are, however, more subtle ways in which these letter-writing campaigns may have had an effect. The first is that the groups provided training to many people in how to file a complaint with the Commission. Some of the other fines issued in the 1990s may have come from people who learned of the requirements for a formal complaint from the groups, but did not credit them in the complaint. This training may also provide people with the knowledge for filing future complaints against stations broadcasting indecency. Although the

---

[1] In Re WUHY-FM, 24 F.C.C.2d 408 (1970) and In Re WGLD-FM, 41 F.C.C.2d 777 (1973).
[2] Paul Farhi, "War of the Words," The Washington Post, 21 May 1995, W12.
[3] Call letters, time of broadcast, and a tape or transcript.

issuance of fines has slowed considerably since the Infinity settlements, stations are still being fined.[4]

Another way in which the American Family Association, in particular, may have used letter-writing campaigns to impact the decision-making process is in exerting pressure on the Commission. Many people, including former FCC Chair Mark Fowler[5] and communications scholar Lucas Powe,[6] saw the April 1987 letters as a "mere alleviation of external pressure."[7] In 1987, Fowler told ADWEEK that he fully expected the Commission's enforcement of indecency to stop with those letters.[8] But, as history has shown, the enforcement increased heavily in the 1990s. Furthermore, the years that saw increasingly larger fines being issued for the violation of the indecency regulations were the same years in which the FCC was inundated with letters sent as a result of AFA's calls to action. While some of this increased enforcement can be traced to other causes, like the nomination hearings discussed below, the possibility that the groups exerted some influence on the Commission cannot entirely be dismissed.

Thus, while concrete measures of success, fines and license revocations, did not result from AFA-driven complaints, it appears that the letters may have had some effect on the regulatory process.

Blocking Renewals and Acquisitions

As described in the previous chapter, the American Family Association and Morality in Media tried on three occasions to convince the FCC that a station

---

[4] For example, see KKND-FM, 1998 FCC LEXIS 3174 (6/29/98), a fine of $6,000 and KBZR-FM, 1998 FCC LEXIS 3073 (6/19/98); a fine of $7,500.
[5] Farhi, "War of Words," W12.
[6] Jr. Powe, Lucas A., "Consistency Over Time: The FCC's Indecency Rerun," Hastings Comm/Ent Law Journal 10 (1988): 571-577.
[7] Powe, "Consistency," 572.
[8] J. Max Robins, "Raunch-Radio Days: Life After the FCC Warnings," ADWEEK, 22 June 1987.

accused of the broadcast of indecent material was not fit to be a licensee. In the first case, WGBH-TV, the station had never been fined for any indecent broadcasts. In the other two cases against the transfer of new licenses to Infinity Broadcasting, the company had been fined several times.

In all three cases the FCC denied the groups' petitions. In the matter of WGBH, decided in 1978, the Commission used the MIM petition to announce that it intended "strictly to observe the narrowness of the Pacifica holding" and had no intention of enforcing the indecency regulations unless a "verbal shock treatment," such as that present in Pacifica, occurred.[9] It was this announcement that heralded nearly a decade of non-enforcement of the indecency policy--something that MIM had definitely not intended.

In the petitions brought against Infinity during its purchases of the Cook-Inlet group in 1992 and KRTH-FM in 1994, the Commission maintained that enforcement proceedings were the place to consider matters of the broadcast of indecent programming.[10] The decisions to fine Infinity on one hand and reward it with new licenses on the other, however, appeared contradictory to some, including some Commissioners.[11] Chairman Sikes dissented from the Cook-Inlet decision, stating that because of the violations of the indecency regulations, he harbored doubts as to Infinity's fitness as a licensee[12] Commissioner Quello, who supported the Cook-Inlet purchase at the end of 1992, opposed the KRTH transfer a little more than a year later.[13] He wrote that the "pattern of egregious repeated violations of FCC indecency rules" made it impossible for him to agree to

---

[9] 69 FCC.2d 1250, 1253.
[10] 8 FCC Rcd 2714, 2714.
[11] David S. Hilzenrath, "FCC Targets Employer of Radio 'Shock Jock;' Agency Delays Infinity Purchase of 3 Stations," The Washington Post, 1 January 1994, B1 and Jason Vest, "FCC to Fine Infinity Over Stern broadcasts; But Firm Allowed to Buy WPGC," The Washington Post, 21 May 1994, D1.
[12] 8 FCC Rcd 2714, 2717-2718.
[13] 9 FCC Rcd 7112, 7116.

giving Infinity yet another license.[14] Despite the opposition of the Commission members, the FCC has consistently taken the position that the broadcast of indecent material, no matter how many times a station is fined, is not, *per se*, a reason to deny a license.

Donald Wildmon had said all along that he wanted to see a license revoked for the broadcast of indecency. He maintained that pulling a license was the only way to block the flow of indecent material.[15] Interestingly, an anonymous source at Infinity told a Washington Post reporter that had the Commission granted the AFA petitions and refused to allow the company to purchase any new licenses, Infinity would have fired Howard Stern.[16]

The idea that Infinity would sacrifice Stern in order to buy more stations is backed up by the decision to settle. In 1995, Infinity settled with the FCC for slightly more than the accrued fines. Infinity had stated all along that it would fight the fines on the grounds of the First Amendment, but the pending removal of the ownership caps on radio prompted Infinity to "normalize" relations with the Commission at any cost.[17] The settlement suggests that Infinity cares more about the bottom line than a First Amendment fight.

The Commission consistently refused to deny a renewal or acquisition of a new license on the grounds of the broadcast of indecent material. Even when Chairman Sikes himself voiced doubts about the wisdom of allowing Infinity to acquire new stations, the Commission continued to deny the petitions of the anti-indecency groups. Thus, the groups' efforts to block the license renewals and

---

[14] 9 FCC Rcd 7112, 7116.

[15] Hearings Before the Committee on Commerce, Science, and Transportation, United States Senate, Alfred C. Sikes, Sherrie P. Marshall, and Andrew C. Barrett, To Be Commissioners, Federal Communications Commission, 101st Cong.,1st. Sess. 392-495 (1989).

[16] Paul Farhi, "Bad Taste, Good Business; To His Employer, Howard Stern Easily Passes a Classic Cost-Benefit Test," The Washington Post, 27 March 1994, H1.

[17] Paul Farhi, "Stern 'Indecency' Case Settled; After 7-year Fight with FCC, Broadcasting Firm to Pay $1.7 Million," The Washington Post, 2 September 1995, F1.

acquisitions of licensees that broadcast indecent material were consistently unsuccessful.

Lobbying and Ex Parte Communication

As Chapter 5 demonstrated, it appears that there was significant contact between the FCC and the American Family Association and Morality in Media immediately preceding the issuance of the April 1987 letters. This lobbying took the form of picketing the Commission headquarters, interpersonal communications in the form of letters and meetings, and a cooperation between the FCC and the groups in the selection of test cases.

There is little doubt that the combination of external pressure represented by the pickets and the internal negotiations were at least partially responsible for the expansion of the FCC's indecency regulation in April 1987. Some believe that the sole purpose of the April letters was to improve Mark Fowler's chances at winning re-nomination.[18] Fowler himself said that the FCC's action on indecency would end with those letters.[19] For the years immediately following the April 1987 action, the FCC's activity regarding the regulation of indecency was minimal, as predicted by Fowler. Therefore, while the groups succeeded in getting the letters sent, nothing much happened. Donald Wildmon responded to the letters by saying "If I were a broadcaster, I'd say anything I wanted to and sleep well as night. . . . The action the FCC took against Stern and that crew has had absolutely no effect."[20]

---

[18] Alex S. Jones, "FCC Studies 'Indecency' on Radio," The New York Times, 22 November 1986, 9.

[19] J. Max Robins, "Raunch-Radio Days: Life After the FCC Warnings," ADWEEK, 22 June 1987, .

[20] J. Max Robins, "Raunch-Radio Days: Life After the FCC Warnings," ADWEEK, 22 June 1987, .

Another of the groups' goals in that time was getting Jack Smith, FCC General Counsel, appointed Chairman of the FCC. They went as far as to ask Pat Buchannan, Reagan's Director of Communications, to ask the president to withdraw his nomination of Dennis Patrick in favor of Smith.[21] As history has shown, this attempt to install an FCC chair sympathetic to the anti-indecency cause was a failure.

Notices of Inquiry and Notices of Proposed Rulemaking

Notices of Inquiry and Proposed Rulemaking provide excellent opportunities for citizen groups to make their positions known to the Commission. The formal comment process allows the groups to cover a range of issues in a forum where they can expect that the comments will be read and considered. Communication scholar Michael McGregor found that the FCC even gave serious consideration to the informal comments submitted in response to NOIs and NPRMs.[22] Because of the level of consideration given comments in the NOI and NPRM process, this represents an excellent opportunity for the groups to impact the decision-making process.

The previous chapter demonstrated that the comments filed by the American Family Association and Morality in Media saturated the 1990 FCC Report on Docket 89-494. It appears that the Commission virtually ignored the industry statistics and information in favor of MIM and AFA. On the surface, that seems to support the notion that the groups exerted an enormous amount of influence on the Commission. But upon careful examination, a different conclusion is apparent. In the 1989 Notice of Inquiry, the FCC put forth a series of "preliminary findings." These findings outlined the reality in which the

---

[21] "Its Official; Patrick for FCC Chairmanship," Broadcasting, 9 February 1987, 43.

Commission believed, namely, that children should be defined as seventeen and under, the broadcast media are pervasive and highly accessible, children use media 24-hours a day, children time-shift with VCRs, children are not supervised in their media usage, channeling and warnings are not effective, and adults have alternative access to indecent material in other media.

Thus, on second look, MIM and AFA did not persuade the Commission to adopt the groups' points of view, they merely provided the data that the Commission wanted to see. Rather than being more influential than the industry, the groups' favored presence in the report is evidence that they gave the Commission support for its own, predetermined positions.

In the areas that the Commission did not already agree with the groups, the comments were ineffective. The Commission ignored MIM's detailed arguments about the erroneous use of children as the primary rationale for the regulation of indecency.[23] The FCC also dismissed MIM's position on the appropriate constitutional test for the regulation on indecency. The AFA comments and reply comments spent a great deal of time discussing evidence of the harm that occurs from exposing children to indecency. The Commission said that all this evidence was pointless because it could regulate without any proof of harm.

Thus, while it *appears* that the MIM and AFA comments were exceedingly persuasive, it also seems that the Commission was really only listening to the evidence that it wanted to hear and agreeing with the conclusions that it already supported. The Commission was not persuaded by any position of AFA or MIM that it had not already supported. Thus, the formal comment process of the Commission was not a place where the groups had any impact on the decision-making process.

---

[22] Michael A. McGregor, "The FCC's Use of Informal Comments in Rule-Making Proceedings," Journal of Broadcasting and Electronic Media 30:4 (1986): 413-425.

Congressional Hearings

The material presented in Chapter 5 demonstrated that the only Congressional hearing in which the groups testified on the matter of broadcast indecency was the nomination hearing for Alfred Sikes, Andrew Barrett, and Sherrie Marshall. That hearing was dominated by talk of increased regulation of the broadcast of indecent material by the subcommittee as well as the three religious and anti-indecency groups who testified.

A few months after those hearings, the Sikes Commission began to actively enforce the indecency regulations, issuing fines to a number of stations. Overall, the Sikes Commission handed down eighteen fines in three years, including the unprecedented $600,000 fine to Infinity. There is little doubt that the regulatory activity of the Commission was, in large part, due to the emphasis that Congress placed on indecency during the nomination hearings of Sikes, Barrett, and Marshall.

The question is, however, how influential was Peggy Coleman's testimony on behalf of the American Family Association and Morality in Media. The three members of the religious and anti-indecency groups that testified had to be invited to the hearing. Nomination hearings, like most congressional committee hearings, are not open chances for any member of the public to speak. Thus, someone on the Communications Subcommittee had to be sympathetic to the group's concerns. The transcript of the hearings shows that a number of senators were quite outspoken on the issue of stepping up enforcement of the indecency regulations. Senator Al Gore, in particular, questioned the nominees closely on the topic, and then voted against them because they did not appear to be completely dedicated to the increased enforcement.[24]

---

[23] This argument also failed to persuade the Commission in the NPRM, Docket 92-223.
[24] Linda Eardley, "Nominee for FCC Advances," St. Louis Post-Dispatch, 2 August 1989, 7A.

Krasnow, Longley, and Terry place Congress in the inner circle of the Broadcast Policy-Making System, along with the FCC and the industry. Congress holds the purse-strings of the Commission, and it also holds advise and consent power over the nominees. Therefore, it is a reasonable assumption that the presence of a representative of AFA and MIM at the Sikes, Barrett, and Marshall hearing was not the key factor in the subsequent enforcement activities of the Sikes Commission. Rather, it is likely that the subcommittee used AFA and MIM as a means to emphasize its members' own agendas. The testimony of Peggy Coleman, alone, would likely not have sent a strong message to the nominees. In contrast, the constant questioning of the future commissioners by the same senators who would be approving their agency's budgets and their own possible re-nominations would convey that message with significant force. Thus, while AFA and MIM's presence certainly did not hurt their goals of increasing the enforcement of indecency, the main impetus for the change in the attitude of the nominees likely came from the senators, not their chosen witnesses.[25]

This research has shown that Morality in Media and the American Family Association have had some successes and some failures in their attempts to impact the decision-making process of the Federal Communications Commission. The last section of this chapter places these conclusions into the context of the Krasnow, Longley, and Terry model.

Krasnow, Longley, and Terry's Model of the Broadcast Policy-Making System

Krasnow, Longley, and Terry view citizen groups as one of the six determiners of broadcast regulation, along with the FCC, the industry, Congress,

[25] Of course, the disposition of the senators may have been affected by the actions of the anti-indecency groups over the years. But since the scope of this study is solely on the groups direct impact on the FCC, any pressure exerted on Congress would be outside the parameters of this research.

the White House, and the courts.[26] In the model of the Broadcast Policy-Making System, the authors place the groups in a weaker position relative to the Commission, the industry, and Congress. In the case studies presented in The Politics of Broadcast Regulation, citizen groups played a variety of roles, albeit subordinate ones. In the final chapter of the book, the authors present tables which describe the activities and inputs of each of the six actors for each of the five case studies.[27] Some of the descriptions mirror the events in the history of the regulation of indecency.

For example, Krasnow, Longley, and Terry describe citizen group participation in one case, the controversy over radio station format changes, as the "major stimulant to the controversy," and seeking "substantial change."[28] These same phrases can be used to describe many of AFA and MIM's actions over the years. The intense lobbying and picketing in 1986 and the massive letter-writing campaign of the 1990s are examples of this. But, like in the case of indecency, citizen groups had little success in the final disposition of the radio format controversy.

Another case study looked at Congress's attempts to rewrite the Communications Act in the late 1970s. In that case, Krasnow, Longley, and Terry describe citizen groups as "involved but ineffective, except on those issues and strategies that coincide with industry."[29] This determination could also be describing the regulation of indecency. In many ways, AFA and MIM were ineffective. They did not get their chosen replacement for Mark Fowler, they were never able to get a station's license revoked or block a transfer, and they

---

[26] Erwin G. Krasnow, Lawrence D. Longley and Herbert A. Terry, The Politics of Broadcast Regulation (New York: St. Martin's Press, 1982), 304.

[27] The five case studies were Format Changes, UHF Television, Limits on Commercials, Comparative License Renewals, and the failed 1970s efforts to rewrite the Communications Act.

[2828] Krasnow, Longley, and Terry, 273.

[29] Krasnow, Longley, and Terry, 277.

were never able to persuade the Commission during rule-making to a position that the Commission did not already hold. However, when the group's goals matched those of one of the central actors in the regulatory process, in this case, Congress, there were successes. The nomination hearings of Sikes, Barrett, and Marshall bear this out. The AFA testimony alone would likely not have sparked the almost immediate actions on indecency by the Sikes Commission. But when the senators themselves took up the calls for increased regulation, the new commissioners reacted in a manner that coincided with the goals of the citizen groups.

AFA and MIM's mixture of successes and failure matches well with the Krasnow, Longley, and Terry model. This research supports the strength of the model in describing long-term policy changes. There is nothing in this research that contradicts the basic validity of the model. Thus, role the citizen groups have played in the regulation of indecency seems to fit with the Krasnow, Longley, and Terry model of the Broadcast Policy-Making System.

Why Do Citizen Groups Fail?

As has been mentioned previously, the question of why citizen groups fail at the FCC is not answered well in the existing research. Most of the research focuses so tightly on presenting the history of the petition to deny and citizen-broadcaster agreement that it ignores the larger question of why the groups' efforts tend to fail. Even those studies that look beyond those two issues ignore the question of why.

Citizen groups are handicapped at the Commission because they are essentially outsiders. The groups do not usually know the language and workings of the FCC in the same way that the regulated industry does. This puts them at a disadvantage. The simple fact of not knowing where the different offices are can interfere with a citizen group's success. Even a group like MIM, who tends to use more insider strategies like the formal comment procedure, remains an outsider in many ways.

Citizen groups are also handicapped by funding and manpower considerations. While the industry views the legal fees paid to those who represent them in front of the FCC as normal operating expenses, a citizen group must make a significant investment to present its view to the Commission.

Finally, the Commission staff may also play a role in the failures of citizen groups. Commissioners and staff alike often use their time at the Commission as a springboard to jobs in the industry. This is known as the revolving door. As a result, it is possible that some staff tend to side with the industry in order to increase the prospects of a subsequent job. In addition, the staff also spend much more time dealing with representatives of the industry, and thus, are more sympathetic to the industry concerns. For these reasons, citizen groups do not see much success at the FCC.

This lack of success by citizen groups is documented by Krasnow, Longley, and Terry in The Politics of Broadcast Regulation. The placement of citizen groups as one of the less powerful actors in the model acknowledges that these groups find little success at the Commission. But the authors do not devote much space to why citizen groups as an actor at the Commission find little success. The Michael McGregor article discussed earlier in the literature review, "The FCC's Use of Informal Comments in Rule-Making Proceedings," found that public comments that were well thought-out and original did find a place in the reports of the Commission. But AFA and MIM, which have spent a great deal of time and money on presenting their views on indecency to the FCC, have been largely unsuccessful in persuading the Commission. This seeming contradiction suggests that further research into this topic is needed.

Suggestions for Further Research

As in any inquiry, this research raised as many questions as it answered. There are several areas of further study that suggest themselves to broaden the base of knowledge about the regulation of indecency. The Krasnow, Longley, and Terry model suggests that citizen groups have ways of influencing the other actors in the model, besides the Commission. A look at how the groups may have attempted to influence Congress, the courts, and the White House and then how those actors, in turn, pressured the FCC would complement and expand the conclusions reached by this research.

Other research could also look into the role of AFA as a licensee in front of the Commission and whether that had any impact on the ability of the group to lobby the Commission. Another question that this research raised is the effect of the industry on the matter of broadcast indecency. Casual observation indicates that the industry was largely silent on the matter of indecency; while it did participate in many areas, the industry did not bring its full weight to bear on the matter. The issue of the industry silence and how this may have affected the ability of the citizen groups to influence the Commission would be an interesting complement to this study.

Finally, a look into whether the personalities and tactics of the groups themselves made the Commission less likely to take their positions seriously. The question of whether there a bias against the conservative groups on the part of the staff of the Commission, or a bias against groups in general would be interesting. Still another question is whether the McGregor findings discussed in the last section are anomalous or do they mean that the Commission is willing to listen to an unorganized public more readily than an organized one. Further research into any of these areas could be another step to a greater understanding of how the Federal Communications Commission regulates and how it is influenced.

References

50 Who Made TV's Landscape; Honed by Pioneers and Visionaries. Advertising Age, 28 February 1995, 44.

Ad Boycott Aimed at Murphy Brown. The Record, 23 July 1992, C16.

Allen, Henry. The Might Controversy; Rodent Hero Accused of Sniffing Cocaine. The Washington Post, 10 June 1988, D1.

Anderson, Susan Heller. Stern's Station Rebuts FCC Charges. The New York Times, 22 December 1986, C16.

Andrews, Edmund L. 2 Views of Decency. The New York Times, 28 December 1992, A12.

Anti-Porn Campaign is Announced by Morality in Media. The Providence Journal-Bulletin, 27 October 1994, 19D.

Baker, C. Edwin. 1996. The Evening Hours During Pacifica Standard Time. Villanova Sports and Entertainment Law Forum 3: 45.

Ballard, Michelle and Milagros Rivera-Sanchez. 1996. Settlement: FCC's Newest Strategy to Address Indecency? Communications and the Law 18 (4): 1-27.

Barton, Richard L. 1976. The Lingering Legacy of Pacifica: Broadcasters' Freedom of Silence. Journalism Quarterly 53 (3): 429-433.

Baughman, James L. 1985. Television's Guardians: The FCC and the Politics of Programming 1958-1967. Knoxville: University of Tennessee Press.

Beard, Betty. New Bid for Circle K Boycott; Religious Group Wants Chain to Halt Sales of 'Porn'. The Arizona Republic, 8 November 1995, A15.

Benkelman, Susan. Decency Test. Newsday, 9 May 1996, A61.

Bensman, Marvin R. 1985. Broadcast Regulation: Selected Cases and Decisions. New York: University Press of America.

Billelo, Suzanne. Her Target: Pornography. Newsday, 19 July 1989, 2.

Blau, Eleanor. Domino's Pulls 'Saturday Night' Ads. The New York Times, 11 April 1989, D25.

Bloom County Comic Strip Angers Religious Leader. The San Diego Union-Tribune, 9 July 1987, A-11.

Boliek, Brooks. Mr. Wildmon Goes to Washington; Longtime Critic of Hollywood Opens Capital Office, Preps Radio Show. The Hollywood Reporter, 21 April 1993.

Brenner, Daniel L. 1982. Censoring the Airwaves: The Supreme Court's Pacifica decision. In Free But Regulated: Conflicting Traditions in Media Law, ed. Daniel L. Brenner and W. L. Rivers:175-180. Ames, IA: Iowa State University Press.

Brenner, Daniel L. The Regulation of Radio and Television in the United States. Media Law & Practice, June, 60-64.

Burden, Jared L. 1987. Tying the Victim's Hands: Curbing Citizen Group Abuse of the Broadcast Licensing Process. Federal Communications Law Journal 39 (October): 259-295.

Burgess, John. FCC to Permit 'Indecency' at Certain Times. The Washington Post, 25 November 1987, E1.

Burgess, John. FCC Fines Missouri TV Station; Penalty is First Under 'Indecency' Rule. The Washington Post, 24 June 1988, D3.

Burgess, John. FCC Presses 'Indecency' Fight; 4 Radio Stations Fined, Other Sent Letters. The Washington Post, A1.

Bush's 3 Nominees for the FCC OK'd by Senate. The San Diego Union-Tribune, 1 August 1989, A-9.

Byers, Mark. Saturday Commentary: Accentuate the Positive in TV; 'Media Watchdogs' Taking Wrong Approach in Efforts to Enforce Morality in Programming. The Daily News of Los Angeles, 14 February 1998, N24.

Caldwell, Deborah Kovach. Disney Under Fire Again. The News and Observer, 7 November 1997, E1.

Caldwell, Deborah Kovach. Dissin' Disney: Boycott Effort Intensifies. News & Record, 28 December 1997, D2.

Cantor, Muriel and Joel Cantor. 1985. United States: A System of Minimal Regulation. In The Politics of Broadcasting, ed. Raymond Kuhn:158-196. New York: St. Martin's Press.

Carlin, John C. 1976. The Rise and Fall of Topless Radio. Journal of Communication Winter: 31-37.

Carman, John. Righteous Reverend Writes Again. The San Francisco Chronicle, 4 April 1994, E1.

Carmode, Ralph Edward. 1986. An Analysis of the Broadcast Policy-Making System an its Application to Federal Communications Commission Docket 20735. Ph.D. Diss., Pennsylvania State University.

Carton, Barbara. Lashing Back at TV Sleaze; Outraged Viewers Gird to Boycott Advertisers. The Boston Globe, 23 April 1989, A1.

Chicurel, Judy. Morality in Media Takes on Adult Stores. The New York Times, 17 June 1990, 12LI -1.

Child's Play on the Net. The Ledger, 30 May 1996, A10.

Christian Group Calls for Boycott of Unilever. Los Angeles Times, 13 June 1995, D3.

Cobb, Nathan. Prime Time Sex; What's Most Surprising About the Increasing Sexual Content of Network TV is that Anyone is Surprised by it at All. The Boston Globe, 30 April 1989, Magazine 20.

Cole, Barry and Mal Oettinger. 1978. Reluctant Regulators: The FCC and the Broadcast Audience. Reading, MA: Addison-Wesley Publishing Company.

Colford Paul D. Another Stern Challenge. Newsday, 31 January 1990, 7.

Communications Media Center. 1977. When Citizens Complain: *UCC v. FCC* A Decade Later. In Mass Communications Law Section Association of American Law Schools:28. New York: Association of American Law Schools and the Communications Media Center.

Conner, Tracy. Jerry Vows He'll Go Down Fighting; Balks at Talk of Easing Up on Sleaze. The New York Post, 2 May 1998, 4.

Conrad, Mark. 1993. With a New President Comes a New FCC Agenda. New York Law Journal January 15: 5.

Conspectus. 1997. Sex, Violence, Children & the Media: Legal, Historical & Empirical Perspectives. CommLaw Conspectus 5 (Summer): 341-358.

Cooper, Cynthia A. 1995. The Role of Congressional Hearings in the Formation of Policy Toward Violence on Television: An Analysis Using the Broadcast Policy-Making System. Ph.D. Diss., University of Tennessee.

Cowan, Geoffrey. 1978. See No Evil. New York: Simon & Schuster.

Cox, James. Rev. Donald Wildmon; Mississippi Minister Takes on TV Networks. USA Today, 17 July 1989, 6B.

Crigler, John and William J. Byrnes. 1989. Decency Redux: The Curious History of the New FCC Broadcast Indecency Policy. Catholic University Law Review 38 (Winter): 329-363.

Dickerson, Marla. Christian Group Escalates Boycott Against Disney. Los Angeles Times, 2 July 1996, D1.

Dobbin, Muriel. Unrelenting Foes Push to Eliminate Arts Agency. Sacramento Bee, 29 June 1997, A1.

Donnerstein, Edward, Barbara Wilson, and Daniel Linz. 1992. On the Regulation of Broadcast Indecency to Protect Children. Journal of Broadcasting & Electronic Media 36: 111-117.

Dorsey, Tom. Is Latest Boycott Fueled by Objectionable TV - Or Fear of Ideas? The Courier-Journal, 10 July 1989, 2C.

Driscoll, Paul. A Return to Safe Harbors? Media Law Notes, 1991, 1+.

Eardley, Linda. More Competition is Goal of Sikes as Head of FCC. St. Louis Post-Dispatch, 8 August 1989, 1B.

Eardley, Linda. Nominee for FCC Advances. St. Louis Post-Dispatch, 2 August 1989, 7A.

Eardley, Linda. Sikes Backs Broadcast Code. St. Louis Post-Dispatch, 1 August 1989, 11A.

Eisner, Marc Allen. 1994. Discovering Patterns in Regulatory History: Continuity, Change and Regulatory Regimes. Journal of Policy History 6: 164.

Elliot, Stuart. Networks are Putting the Pressure on Pressure Groups. The New York Times, 1 August 1991, D17.

Elliot, Stuart. A Hit Prime-Time Show Without Most Mainstream Advertisers? Dial 'NYPD Blue'. The New York Times, 2 November 1993, D20.

Emord, Jonathan W. 1991. Freedom, Technology, and the First Amendment. San Francisco: Pacific Research Institute for Public Policy.

Family Group Attacks Disney Music. The Washington Times, 3 July 1997, B7.

Farhi, Paul. FCC Bans All 'Indecent' Broadcasts; Agency: Move Taken to Protect Children. The Washington Post, 13 July 1990, A1.

Farhi, Paul. FCC 'Indecency' Rule on Trial; Constitutionality of Radio and TV Restriction at Issue. The Washington Post, 28 January 1991, B1.

Farhi, Paul. Indecency Ban by FCC Overturned; Broadcast Standard Unconstitutionally Vague,' Court Rules. The Washington Post, 18 May 1991, A1.

Farhi, Paul. FCC Fines Station $105,000 Over Stern; Largest-Ever Penalty for 'Indecent' Broadcast. The Washington Post, 28 October 1992, D1.

Farhi, Paul. FCC to Levy Stiff Fine Over Stern; Agency Seeks $600,000 from Three Stations. The Washington Post, 18 December 1992, D1.

Farhi, Paul. FCC's Stern Punishment; Radio Group to be Fined, Purchases May be Delayed. The Washington Post, 25 November 1992, E1.

Farhi, Paul. FCC's Stern Rebuke; Infinity Unrepentant; Harsher Actions Loom. The Washington Post, 19 December 1992, D1.

Farhi, Paul. FCC to Still Enforce Curbs on 'Indecency;' Broadcast Ban Hours Cut After Court Ruling. The Washington Post, 25 November 1993, D1.

Farhi, Paul. 'Indecency' Regulations overturned; Court Says FCC's Curb on Broadcasting is Unconstitutional. The Washington Post, 24 November 1993, A1.

Farhi, Paul. Stern Gets Some Shock Treatment; Fined Again, Company Reins in Disc Jockey. The Washington Post, 13 August 1993, D1.

Farhi, Paul. Bad Taste, Good Business; To His Employer, Howard Stern Easily Passes a Classic Cost-Benefit Test. The Washington Post, 27 March 1994, H1.

Farhi, Paul. FCC Still Weighting Decision on Infinity Broadcasting's Purchase. The Washington Post, 6 January 1994, D11.

Farhi, Paul. Stern, Firm Said to Avoid Stiff Penalty. The Washington Post, 28 January 1994, G2.

Farhi, Paul. Stern 'Indecency' Case Settled; After 7-year Fight with FCC, Broadcasting Firm to Pay $1.7 Million. The Washington Post, 2 September 1995, F1.

Farhi, Paul War of the Words. The Washington Post, 21 May 1995, W12.

Farhi, Paul. Top 2 Radio Station Operators to Merge in $4.9 Billion Deal. The Washington Post, 21 June 1996, A1.

FCC Censorship Role Rejected. Facts on File World Digest, 4 August 1978, 599 E1.

FCC Indecency Ban Goes to Court. Broadcasting, 9 January 1989, 70.

FCC Targets 3 Over Indecency on Radio Waves. The San Diego Union-Tribune, 25 August 1989, A-6.

Feldman, Charles and Stanley Tickton. 1976. Obscene/Indecent Programming: Regulation of Ambiguity. Journal of Broadcasting 20 (2): 273-281.

Feldman, Paul J. 1990. The FCC and Regulation of Broadcast Indecency: Is There a National Broadcast Standard in the Audience? Federal Communications Law Journal 41 (3): 369-400.

Fife, Marilyn Diane. 1983. FCC Policy on Minority Ownership in Broadcasting: A Political Systems Analysis of Regulatory Policymaking. Ph.D. Diss., Stanford University.

Filtering Airwaves for Indecency. The New York Times, 1 November 1987, 65.

Foe of Adult Magazines Tries to Enter Court Case. The San Diego Union-Tribune, 6 June 1986, A-16.Flint, Joe. Survey Finds Less Raciness. Daily Variety, 26 December 1996, 1.

Fowler, Mark S. and Daniel L. Brenner. 1982. A Marketplace Approach to Broadcast Regulation. Texas Law Review 60: 207.

Garay, Ronald. 1978. Access: Evolution of the Citizen Agreement. Journal of Broadcasting 22 (1): 95-106.

Garbus, Martin and David Y. Atlas. Private Censorship is Uniquely Dangerous. The National Law Journal, 25 March 1996, A21.

Gay, Verne. Group Targets 'Absolute Strangers'. Newsday, 18 March 1991, 53.

Gayoso, Jay A. 1989. The FCC's Regulation of Broadcast Indecency: A Broadened Approach for Removing Immorality from the Airwaves. University of Miami Law Review 43: 871-919.

Gerard, Jeremy. Enough Ads are Expected for NBC's Abortion Film. The New York Times, 12 May 1989, D15.

Gerhart, Ann and Annie Groer. The Reliable Source; Raising the Bawdy Count. The Washington Post, 18 October 1996, D3.

Gibson, William E. Preacher's Campaign for Anti-porn Law Slows Effort to Pass It; Phone Calls, Letters Swamp Bill's Sponsor. The Orange County Register, 26 June 1988, A21.

Gillmor Don M., Jerome A. Barron, T. F. Simon, and Herbert A. Terry. 1990. The Regulation of Electronic Media. In Mass Communications Law: Cases and Comment:825-828. St. Paul: West Publishing Company.

Glasser, Theodore L. and Harvey Jassem. 1980. Indecent Broadcasts and the Listener's Right of Privacy. Journal of Broadcasting 24 (3): 285-299.

Goldsamt, Seth T. 1995. "Crucified by the FCC"? Howard Stern, the FCC, and Selective Prosecution. Columbia Journal of Law and Social Problems 28: 203.

Graham Renee. Morality's Defenders or Freedom's Enemies? The Boston Globe, 6 August 1990, Metro/Region 13.

Group Protests Playboy Videos. The Orlando Sentinel, 25 October 1994, C3.

Group to Gauge TV Smut, Seek Sponsor Boycotts. The Christian Science Monitor, 3 February 1981, 2.

Groups Join Baptist Boycott of Disney. The Advocate, 13 July 1996, 1E.

Grundfest, Joseph A. 1976. Citizen Participation in Broadcast Licensing Before the FCC. Santa Monica, CA: The Rand Corporation, with help from a grant from the Markle Foundation.

Guimary, Donald L. 1975. Citizens' Groups and Broadcasting. Praeger Special Studies in U.S. Economic, Social, and Political Issues. New York: Praeger Publishers.

Hammond, Allen S. 1996. Indecent Proposals: Reason, Restraint And Responsibility In The Regulation Of Indecency. Villanova Sports and Entertainment Law Forum 3: 259.

Hanafin, Teresa M. Convent to Court; In Between, New Judge Defended Adult-Book Sellers. The Boston Globe, 3 May 1992, 29.

Harden, Mike. Pornography Lurks Almost Everywhere in Watchdog's Eyes. The Columbus Dispatch, 14 January 1998, 1E.

Harrington, Richard. Howard Stern; All Id, No Lid; He's Raunchy and Ranting. But is He Sick or Slick? The Washington Post, 28 October 1993, D1.

Hartigan, Patty. Group Takes on Obscenity Law. The Boston Globe, 8 March 1991, Arts & Film 29.

Hatch, Blanch. Fight Pornography. Chicago Daily Herald, 26 October 1997, 16.

Havick, John J., ed. 1983. Communications Policy and the Political Process. Edited by Bernard K. Johnpoll. Contributions in Political Science. Westport, CT: Greenwood Press.

Hentoff, Nat. Censors of the Airwaves. The Washington Post, 6 March 1993, A21.

Hilliard, Robert L. 1991. The Federal Communications Commission: A Primer. Stoneham, MA: Butterworth-Heimnemann.

Hilzenrath, David S. FCC Targets Employer of Radio 'Shock Jock;' Agency Delays Infinity Purchase of 3 Stations. The Washington Post, 1 January 1994, B1.

Hiscock, John. Ellen is Out of the Closet and Out of the Door. The Daily Telegraph, 25 April 1998, 3.

Hoffman, David. Reagan Hears Pleas to Battle Pornography. The Washington Post, 29 March 1983, A5.

Hsiung, James C. 1987. Indecent Broadcast: An Assessment of Pacifica's Impact. Communications and the Law February: 41-56.

Huffman, John L. and Denise M. Trauth. 1991. Obscenity, Indecency, and the Rehnquist Court. Communications and the Law March: 3-23.

Its Official; Patrick for FCC Chairmanship. Broadcasting, 9 February 1987, 43.

Jassem, Harvey and Theodore L. Glasser. 1983. Children, Indecency and the Perils of Broadcasting: The 'Scared Straight' Case. Journalism Quarterly 60 (3): 509-512.

Jeffreys, Daniel. Stateside. The Independent, 20 June 1995, 16.

Jeffreys, Daniel. When a Wildmon Wreaks Havoc; The White Knight of American Family Values Knows No Limits When Pitted Against Big Business. The Independent, 27 July 1995, Life 6.

Jones, Alex S. FCC Studies 'Indecency' on Radio. The New York Times, 22 November 1986, 9.

Kerrigan, Wade. 1993. NOTE: FCC Regulation of the Radio Industry: A Safe Harbor for Indecent Programming? Iowa Law Review 79: 143.

A Kick in the Pants. Star Tribune, 20 May 1992, 2D.

Kim, Haeryon. 1990. The Politics of Broadcast Deregulation: Beyond Krasnow, Longley, and Terry's 'Broadcast Policy-making System". Presented at Association for Education in Journalism and Mass Communication. Minneapolis, Minnesota.

Kim, Haeryon. 1992. Theorizing Deregulation: An Exploration of the Utility of the 'Broadcast Policy-Making System' Model. Journal of Broadcasting & Electronic Media 36 (2): 153-173.

Kim, Haeryon. 1993. Congressional Influence on the FCC: An Analysis of Confirmation hearings for Commission Chairmen, 1969-1989. Communications and the Law 15 (4): 37-54.

Kim, Haeryon. 1995. The Politics of Deregulation: Public Participation in the FCC Rulemaking Process for DBS. Telecommunications Policy 19 (1): 51-60.

Klingeman, Henry. Fowler Play, Renomination of FCC Chairman Mark Fowler. National Review, 21 November 1986, 30.

Kornhauser, Anne. Chairman Patrick's Confidante; FCC's Dianne Killory Eyes Active Role. Legal Times, 4 May 1987, 4.

Kowet, Don. The 'Righteous Indignation' of Donald Wildmon; How a Mississippi Minister Terrorizes the TV Networks. The Washington Times, 12 July 1989, E1.

Krasnow, Erwin G. The Politics of Program Regulation. Broadcasting, 2 November 1987, 28.

Krasnow, Erwin G., Harry F. Cole, and William E. Kennard. 1983. FCC Regulation and Other Oxymorons: Seven Axioms to Grind. Hastings Comm/Ent Law Journal 5 (4): 759-777.

Krasnow, Erwin G., Lawrence D. Longley, and Herbert A. Terry. 1982. The Politics of Broadcast Regulation. New York: St. Martin's Press.

Kropp, Arthur J. Beware Anti-Gay Campaign. The Plain Dealer, 9 June 1994, 11B.

Labunski, Richard E. 1981. The First Amendment Under Siege: The Politics of Broadcast Regulation. Edited by Bernard K. Johnpoll. Contributions in Political Science. Westport, CT: Greenwood Press.

Lander, Estelle. Advertisers Get the Squeeze. New York Newsday, 17 April 1989, 1.

Lev, Michael. A Conservative Group Sends Boycott Warning. The New York Times, 15 July 1991, D9.

Levin, Gary. Wildmon Boycott Sparks Unilever Second Thoughts. Daily Variety, 3 July 1995, 3.

Lewis, Cherie Sue. 1986. Television License Renewal Challenges by Women's Groups. Ph.D. Diss., University of Minnesota.

Linker, Jan Helene. 1981. Public Intervenors and the Public Airwaves: The Effect of Interest Groups on Federal Communications Commission Decisions. Ph.D. Diss., Emory University.

Linker, Jan Helene. 1983. Public Intervenors and the Public Airwaves: The Effect of Interest Groups on Federal Communications Commission Decisions. In Communications Policy and the Political Process, ed. John J. Havick:223. Westport, CT: Greenwood Press.

Lipschultz, Jeremy Harris. 1992. Conceptual Problems of Broadcast Indecency Policy and Application. Communications and the Law June: 3-29.

Lipschultz, Jeremy Harris. 1993. The Function of Audience and Community Feedback in Broadcast Indecency Complaints and Station Management Responses: A Comparative Case Study of WLUP-AM and KSJO-FM. Communications and the Law 15 (2): 17-42.

Lipschultz, Jeremy Harris. 1996. The Influence of the United States Court of Appeals for the District of Columbia Circuit on Broadcast Indecency Policy. Villanova Sports and Entertainment Law Forum 3: 65.

Lipson, Karin. Artist Sues Conservative Group. Newsday, 22 May 1990, 5.

Longley, Lawrence D., Erwin G. Krasnow, and Herbert A. Terry. 1982. The Courts in Broadcast Regulatory Policy-Making. Hastings Comm/Ent Law Journal 4 (3): 377-388.

Longley, Lawrence D., Herbert A. Terry, and Erwin G. Krasnow. 1983. Citizens Groups in Broadcast Regulatory Policy-Making. Policy Studies Journal 12 (2): 258-270.

Louv, Richard. In Moral Marketing, Statistics Don't Count for Much. The San Diego Union-Tribune, 11 May 1986, A-3.

Lowe, Roger K. Two Sides of War Over Decency Standards to Have Final Hearing. The Columbus Dispatch, 29 March 1998, 1D.

Lyke, M. L. Online Smut: Too Easy for Kids to Find?; Pornography: An Innocent Search Can Lead Children to X-Rated Web Sites. The Baltimore Sun, 4 May 1998, 3C.

Mahan, Elizabeth and Jorge Reina Schement. 1984. The Broadcast Regulatory Process: Toward a New Analytical Framework. In Progress in Communication Sciences, ed. Brenda Dervin and Melvin J. Voigt, IV:1-22. Norwood, NJ: ABLEX Publishing Corporation.

Mallory, Jim. Group Threatens Suit to Force Book's Removal. The Denver Post, 30 April 1997, B-3.

Masters, Kim. Arts Agency Chairman Defends Film Grant; 'Poison' Not Obscene, NEA's Frohnmayer Says. The Washington Post, 30 March 1991, C1.

Mayer, Caroline E. FCC Curbs Radio, TV Language; Agency Threatens Stations that are Sexually Explicit. The Washington Post, 17 April 1987, A1.

McDougal, Dennis. FCC Versus Howard Stern: Agency's 'Indecency' Ruling Hasn't Stopped N.Y. Deejay. Los Angeles Times, 19 August 1987, 6-1.

McDougal, Dennis. FCC Won't Back Off From April Indecency Ruling; More Explicit Programming After Midnight. Los Angeles Times, 25 November 1987, 6-1.

McDougal, Dennis. Radio Daze: FCC Moves Indecency Issue to Front Burner. Los Angeles Times, 17 August 1987, 6-1.

McDougal, Dennis. At Issue: 'Indecency' Still Murky Issue. Los Angeles Times, 19 February 1988, Part 6-1.

McDougal, Dennis. Obscenity Issue Still Unresolved. Los Angeles Times, 4 January 1988, 6-1.

McDougal, Dennis. U.S. Likened to Iran on Free Speech. The Record, 29 March 1989, E16.

McDougal, Dennis. TV Boycott Fails to Dent Tuesday Ratings. Los Angeles Times, 31 October 1991, F5.

McGregor, Michael A. 1986. The FCC's Use of Informal Comments in Rule-Making Proceedings. Journal of Broadcasting and Electronic Media 30 (4): 413-425.

McManus, Michael J. Organization Flexes Muscle Against Porn with Journal. The Fresno Bee, 19 April 1997, C7.

McMillar, Colleen. Adult Video Tougher to Find With New Laws. The Times-Picayune, 25 January 1993, B2.

Mermigas, Diane. 'Roe' Loses Ads; NBC Stands Firm. Electronic Media, 15 May 1989, 3.

Midnight Blue; An FCC Time Limit for Raunch. Time, 7 December 1987, 61.

Miller, Jerry. Pornography Assailed by Morality in media President at Forum. The Union Leader, 26 July 1993, 6.

Millman, Nancy. Missing the Mark; Wildmon's Battle with TV a Big Zero, Experts Say. Chicago Tribune, 12 April 1994, Tempo 2.

Molotsky, Irvin. FCC Rules on Indecent Programming. The New York Times, 25 November 1987, C25.

Monday, Mark. Adult-Magazine Sales Stir Handful of Pickets at 2 South County Stores. The San Diego Union-Tribune, 20 April 1989, B-18.

Mosco, Vincent. 1979. Broadcasting in the United States: Innovative Challenge and Organization Control. Edited by Melvin J. Voigt. Communication and Information Science. Norwood, NJ: Ablex Publishing Corporation.

'Mother Jones' Calls Wildmon a Paper Tiger. Orlando Sentinel Tribune, 24 October 1992, D7.

Myerson, Allen R. A Texas Paper in a Dispute Over Gay Editor. The New York Times, 29 January 1996, D1.

The Nation. Los Angeles Times, 19 April 1987, 2.

National Obscenity Law Center Created. The New York Times, 2 September 1976, 33.

New York Report. WWD, 2 November 1995, 6.

Newsbites. The Orange County Register, 17 September 1987, K2.

Nord, David Paul. 1978. The FCC, Educational Broadcasting, and Political Interest Group Activity. Journal of Broadcasting 22 (3): 321-338.

Notes on People; Morality Campaign. The New York Times, 10 September 1981, B4.

Nugent, Robert V. Kmart's Earnings. Los Angeles Times, 26 March 1995, D2.

O'Brien, Barbara. Spice Fare is Obscene, Group Told; Leader of Morality in Media Asks Action. The Buffalo News, 28 October 1993, Local Page.

O'Harrow, Robert. Fairfax School Board Rejects Appeal for Textbook Disclaimer; Parents Found Creationism Reference Demeaning. The Washington Post, 30 May 1997, D6.

O'Steen, Kathleen. Wildmon Loses Round in Docu Suit. Daily Variety, 10 September 1992, 1.

O'Steen, Kathleen. Wildmon Spends Big Ad Bucks Against H'Wood. Daily Variety, 2 December 1992, 8.

Parachini, Allan and Dennis McDougal. Art in the Eighties; Censorship: A Decade of Tighter Control of the Arts. Los Angeles Times, 25 December 1989, F1.

Parachini, Allan and Dennis McDougal. Censorship and the Arts Reach Boiling Point. Los Angeles Times, 18 June 1990, F1.

Pasztor, David. Lean to the Left, Lean to the Right; The Star-Telegram Struggles to Please. Dallas Observer, 9 May 1996.

Peters, Robert W. 1994. Information Superhighway or Technological Sewer: What Will It Be? Federal Communication Law Journal 47 (December): 333-338.

Peyser, Andrea. Obscenity of Censors Taints Art of 'Lolita'. The New York Post, 7 May 1998, 24.

Powe, Jr., Lucas A. 1988. Consistency Over Time: The FCC's Indecency Rerun. Hastings Comm/Ent Law Journal 10: 571-577.

Powe, Lucas A. 1987. American Broadcasting and the First Amendment. Berkeley: University of California Press.

President Reagan. Facts on File World Digest, 3 June 1983, 408 G2.

Pressure Group Claims Success. St. Petersburg Times, 9 July 1998, 7E.

Price, Joyce. Conservative Coalition Targets Nominee for Surgeon General. The Washington Times, 27 June 1993, A1.

Protecting Traditional Marriage. The Indianapolis Star, 14 June 1996, D2.

Pugh, Jeanne. Boycott of 'Last Temptation' a Shadow of Deeper Threat. St. Petersburg Times, 27 August 1988, 2E.

Racy DJ Gets WXRK in Trouble. The Record, 18 November 1986, A1.

Rally Planned to Protest Health Textbooks' Approval. Austin American-Statesman, 5 January 1994, B3.

Ralston in 'Saturday Night' Flap. St. Louis Post-Dispatch, 17 March 1989, 13D.

Ray, William B. 1990. FCC: The Ups and Downs of Radio-TV Regulation. Ames: Iowa State University Press.

Reed, Julia. Raunch 'n' Roll Radio is Here to Stay. U.S. News and World Report, 4 May 1987, 52.

Reilly, Joseph J. Keep the Airwaves Clean. Newsday, 4 February 1990, 2.

Rev. Morton Hill, 68, Pornography Opponent. Chicago Tribune, 7 November 1985, Chicagoland 10.

The Rev. Morton Hill; Led Pornography Foes. The New York Times, 6 November 1985, D27.Richmond, Ray. When Consumers Talk, Sponsors Listen. The Orange County Register, 9 April 1989, L28.

Richmond, Ray. Morality in Media Rips TV Rating Plan. Daily Variety, 5 December 1996, 5.

Rippel, Amy C. Critics Undress Law Over Strip Club. Port St. Lucie News, 22 July 1996, B1.

Rivera-Sanchez, Milagros. 1993. The Regulatory History of Broadcast Indecency, 1907-1987. Ph.D. Diss., University of Florida.

Rivera-Sanchez, Milagros. 1994. Developing an Indecency Standard: The Federal Communications Commission and the Regulation of Offensive Speech, 1927-1964. Journalism History 20 (1): 3-14.

Rivera-Sanchez, Milagros. 1997. How Far is Too Far? The Line Between 'Offensive' and 'Indecent' Speech. Federal Communications Law Journal 49 (2): 327-366.

Rivera-Sanchez, Milagros and Michelle Ballard. 1998. A Decade of Indecency Enforcement: A Study of How the FCC Assesses Indecency Fines (1987-1997). Journalism Quarterly 75 (1): 143-153.

Robins, J. Max. Raunch-Radio Days: Life After the FCC Warnings. ADWEEK, 22 June 1987.

Rogers, Kathryn. 'Morality in Media' Targets TV; Fight 'Sleaze' by Turning Off Sets All Day on Friday, Group Urges. St. Louis Dispatch, 10 February 1994, 4A.

Rogers, Lois M. Return to Family Values Waretown Man's Mission. Asbury Park Press, 5 July 1995, G10.

Rogers, Lois M. Events to Celebrate National Prayer Day. Asbury Park Press, 1 May 1996, B5.

Rosenfeld, Megan. The Battle for Prime-Time Decency; The National Federal for Decency's Battle with Prime-Time Television. The Washington Post, 3 February 1981, B1.

Ruggieri, Melissa. Sex-show Host Won't Be Cowed by Opponents. Sun-Sentinel, 22 March 1995, 3E.

Sachs, Andrea. Kiddie Porn or Bad Taste?; AFA's Trueman Says Jeans Ads Cross Legal Line. Advertising Age, 18 September 1995, 52.

Sadler, Roger L. 1992. The Federal Communications Commission and the Regulation of Indecency, The Evolution of the Concept of Chilling Effects. Ph.D. Diss., Indiana University.

Samoriski, Jan H., John L. Huffman, and Denise M. Trauth. 1995. Indecency, the Federal Communications Commission, and the Post-Sikes Era: A Framework for Regulation. Journal of Broadcasting & Electronic Media 39: 51-72.

Saturday Ticker. Chicago Tribune, 21 October 1989, Business 8.

Sawyers, Arlena. Group Launches Boycott of Chrysler, Cites Playboy Ads. Automotive News, 14 January 1991, 3.

Schmich, Mary T. The Gospel on Trash TV; Rev. Donald Wildmon Feels Called to Make the Networks Pay. Chicago Tribune, 22 May 1989, Tempo 1.

Schrier, Helene T. 1990. A Solution to Indecency on the Airwaves. Federal Communication Law Journal 41 (1): 69-107.

Schwartz, Tony. 400 Rightist Groups in National Coalition to Start Boycott of TV; Wildmon Sponsors This Week. The New York Times, 22 January 1981, A12.

Seba, Erwin. Smut-Fighter Gaining Access to Wichita with Station Buy. Wichita Business Journal, 10 June 1994, 1.

Seel, Peter Benjamin. 1995. High-Definition Television and United States Telecommunication Policy. Ph.D. Diss., Indiana University.

Selcraig, Bruce. America's Art Critic. St. Petersburg Times, 6 October 1990, 4E.

Selcraig, Bruce. Reverend Wildmon's War of the Arts. The New York Times, 2 September 1990, 22.

Shales, Tom. Tony Randall for the Defense; The Series and the Fury; A Furor Over NBC's New 'Love, Sidney'. The Washington Post, 7 July 1981, C1.

Shales, Tom. On the Air; Attack of the TV Reformers; The Aftermath of a Season. The Washington Post, 25 June 1989, G1.

Sheinfeld, Lois P. FCC Doublespeak. Film Comment, September/October, 87-90.

Slavin, Sarah and M. Stephen Pendleton. 1983. Feminism and the FCC. In Communications Policy and the Political Process, ed. John J. Havick:223. Westport, CT: Greenwood Press.

Sloan, Pat and Jennifer DeCoursey. Klein's Risqué Jean Ads Dodge Kiddie Porn Rap from the Feds. Advertising Age, 20 November 1995, 25.

Smith, F. Leslie. 1979. The Charlie Walker Case. Journal of Broadcasting 23 (2): 137-151.

Smolla, Rodney A. 1992. Free Speech in an Open Society. New York: Alfred A. Knopf.

Stein, Joe. A Rundown of Pressure Groups Who Seek to Influence TV. The San Diego Union-Tribune, 14 July 1989, C-15.

Stern, Christopher. Content Controversy Goes 'South'. Variety, 18 August 1997, 21.

Suit Seeks to Halt Campaign Against 'Adult' Magazine Sales. St. Louis Post-Dispatch, 2 November 1989, 15A.

Sukow, R. House Passes 6 a.m.-Midnight Ban. Broadcasting, 10 August 1992, 28.

Swerdlow, Joel. The Great American Crusade in Televisionland. The Washington Post, 7 June 1981, K1.

Takahama, Valerie. Sex, Violence; Thousands of Angry Viewers Join 'Turn Off TV Day'. The Orange County Register, 30 October 1991, B7.

Terry, Herbert A. and Erwin G. Krasnow. 1992. In Defense of the 'Broadcasting Policy-Making System' Model. Journal of Broadcasting and Electronic Media 36 (4): 479-480.

Thomas, Pierre and Paul Farhi. Calvin Klein Ads Cleared. The Washington Post, 16 November 1995, D7.

Treaster, Joseph B. TV Advertisers Meet Coalition in Effort to Avoid Boycott. The New York Times, 26 June 1981, A10.

Tucker, David E. and Jeffrey Saffelle. 1982. The Federal Communications Commission and the Regulation of Children's Television. Journal of Broadcasting 26 (3): 657-669.

Turkington, Richard C. 1996. Safe Harbors and Stern Warnings: FCC Regulation of Indecent Broadcasting. Villanova Sports and Entertainment Law Forum 3: 1-13.

TV's Ellen Controversy Expected to Continue Actress to be on News Show Friday. The Dallas Morning News, 25 April 1997, 4B.

Tyrer, Thomas. 'Murphy' Sponsors Targets for Boycott. Electronic Media, 27 July 1992, 4.

Vest, Jason. FCC to Fine Infinity Over Stern broadcasts; But Firm Allowed to Buy WPGC. The Washington Post, 21 May 1994, D1.

Volland, Victor. Video Stores have 'Priest'; Groups Protest. St. Louis Post-Dispatch, 27 January 1996, 5D.

Watchdog group: Violence on TV Rises Significantly. The Des Moines Register, 6 September 1995, 5.

Walter, Tom. TV Strikes Gold with 'Crude'. The Commercial Appeal, 8 March 1998 E1.

Weaver, Warren. Justice Department Reverses Stance on Indecency. The New York Times, 1 April 1978, 14.

Weinberg, Jonathan. 1996. Vagueness and Indecency. Villanova Sports and Entertainment Law Forum 3: 221.

Weinstein, Steve. How 'Jerker' Helped Ignite Obscenity Debate; Comedian Carlin has a Few Choice Words for Media Watchdogs. Los Angeles Times, 18 August 1987, 6-1.

Werner, Ben. The Adventures of Ozzy and Marilyn. The Orange County Register, 27 June 1997, F10.

Wesolowski, James Walter. 1969. Obscene, Indecent, or Profane Broadcast Language as Construed by the Federal Courts. Journal of Broadcasting 13 (2): 203-219.

White, Gayle. Southern Baptists vs. Disney; Is the Boycott Working? The Atlanta Journal and Constitution, 7 March 1998, O1.

Wildmon Calls for Boycott of Levi's Because Levi's in Boycotting Scouts. The Atlanta Journal-Constitution, 19 May 1992, A3.

Wildmon Threatens Boycott over 'Temptation'. The San Diego Union-Tribune, 15 July 1988, C-11.

Wildmon, Donald. 1989. Don Wildmon: The Man the Networks Love to Hate. Wilmore, KY: Bristol Books.

Wildmon, Don. Book Excerpt: 'Don Wildmon'. Electronic Media, 8 January 1990, 89.

Wildmon, Donald E. Protect the Right to Boycott Pornography. USA Today, 25 April 1990, 10A.

Wiley, Richard. 1988. The Independence of Independent Agencies: Political Influence at the FCC. Duke Law Journal April/June: 280.

Williams, Wenmouth. 1976. Impact of Commissioner Background on FCC Decisions: 1962-1975. Journal of Broadcasting 20 (2): 239-260.

Wing, Susan. 1978. Morality and Broadcasting: FCC Control of 'Indecent' Material Following *Pacifica*. Federal Communications Law Journal 31 (1): 145-173.

Wise, Edythe. 1996. A Historical Perspective on the Protection of Children From Broadcast Indecency. Villanova Sports and Entertainment Law Forum 3: 15-43.

Wolfe, Bill. Minister Finds Support in Drive to Clean Up TV. The Courier-Journal, 5 August 1989, 5A.

Wolff, Craig. Mighty Mouse Flying High on Flowers. The New York Times, 26 July 1988, B1.

Wollert, James Alvin. 1976. Regulatory Decision-Making: The Federal Communications Commission (1966-1975). Ph.D. Diss., Michigan State University.

Yorke, Jeffrey. On the Dial; FCC Cites Stern for Indecency. The Washington Post, 4 December 1990, D7.

Yorke, Jeffrey. 'Smut' Inquiry Spreading; FCC Probes WJFK's Airing of 'Howard Stern Show'. The Washington Post, 3 November 1992, C7.

Yorke, Jeffrey. Stern Talk Results in Fine. The Washington Post, 27 October 1992, C7.

Zeidenberg, Leonard. Indecency: Radio's Sound, FCC's Fury. Broadcasting, 22 June 1987, 46.

Document Reference List

FCC Documents

Commission Announces Action on 95 Indecency Complaints, 1989 FCC LEXIS 2317 (1989).

Enforcement of Prohibitions Against Broadcast Obscenity and Indecency, 4 FCC Rcd 457 (1988).

In re Apparent Liability of Station WGLD-FM, 41 FCC.2d 919 (1973).

In re Applications of E.G. Robinson, Jr. as Palmetto Broadcasting Company for renewal of license, 33 FCC 250 (1961).

In re Applications of E.G. Robinson, Jr. as Palmetto Broadcasting Company for renewal of license, 33 FCC 265 (1961).

In re Application of Jack Straw Memorial Foundation, 21 FCC.2d 833 (1970).

In re Application of Jack Straw Memorial Foundation, 26 FCC.2d 97 (1970).

In re Application of Jack Straw Memorial Foundation, 29 FCC.2d 334 (1971).

In re Applications of Pacifica Foundation, 1 Rad. Reg.2d (P& F) 747 (1964).

In re Applications of Pacifica Foundation, 6 Rad. Reg.2d 570 (1965).

In re Applications of Pacifica Foundation, 16 FCC.2d 712 (1969).

In re Application of Trustees of the University of Pennsylvania, 57 FCC.2d 793 (1976).

In re Application of Trustees of the University of Pennsylvania, 70 FCC.2d 1017 (1977).

In re Application of Trustees of the University of Pennsylvania, 69 FCC.2d 1394 (1978).

In re Application of Trustees of the University of Pennsylvania, 71 FCC.2d 416 (1979).

In Re Application of WGBH Educational Foundation for Renewal of License for Non Commercial Education Station WGBH-TV, 69 FCC.2d 1250 (1978).

In re Notice to Trustees of the University of Pennsylvania of Apparent Liability for Forfeiture, 57 FCC.2d 782 (1975).

In Re WUHY-FM, 24 F.C.C.2d 408 (1970).

In the Matter of a Citizen's Complaint Against Pacifica Foundation Station WBAI, 56 FCC.2d 94 (1975).

In the Matter of Enforcement of Prohibitions Against Broadcast Indecency in 18 U.S.C. @1464, 4 FCC Rcd 8358 (1989).

In the Matter of Enforcement of Prohibitions Against Broadcast Indecency in 18 U.S.C. @1464, 5 FCC Rcd 5297 (1990).

In the Matter of Enforcement of Prohibitions Against Broadcast Indecency in 18 U.S.C. @1464, 8 FCC Rcd 704 (1993).

In the Matter of Infinity Broadcasting, 2 FCC Rcd 2705 (1987).

In the Matter of Infinity Broadcasting; In the Matter of Pacifica Foundation, Inc; In the Matter of The Regents of the University of California, 3 FCC Rcd 930 (1987).

In the Matter of Kansas City Television, 4 FCC Rcd 7653 (1988).

In the Matter of Pacifica Foundation, Inc, 2 FCC Rcd 2698 (1987).

In the Matter of Sagittarius Broadcasting Corporation, 10 FCC Rcd 12245 (1995).

In the Matter of The Regents of the University of California, 2 FCC Rcd 2703 (1987).

In the Matter of the Renewal of the License of Station KRAB-FM, 24 FCC.2d 266 (1970).

In the Matter of Sonderling Broadcasting, 41 F.C.C.2d 777 (1973).

KCNA-FM, 6 FCC Rcd 2174 (1991).

KFBI-FM, 8 FCC Rcd 6790 (1993).

KFBI-FM, 9 FCC Rcd 1753 (1994).

KFI-AM, 6 FCC Rcd 3699 (1989).

KFMH-FM, 9 FCC Rcd 1681 (1994).

KGB-FM, 7 FCC Rcd 3207 (1992).

KKLZ-FM, 9 FCC Rcd 4454 (1994).

KLOL-FM, 5 FCC Rcd 6332 (1990).

KLOL-FM, 8 FCC Rcd 3228 (1993).

KLUC-FM 6 FCC Rcd 3706 (1989).

KMEL-FM, 7 FCC Rcd 4857 (1992).

KNON-FM, 9 FCC Rcd 1679 (1994).

KSD-FM, 6 FCC Rcd 3689 (1990).

KSJO-FM, 5 FCC Rcd 3821 (1990).

KSLX-FM, 7 FCC Rcd 7321 (1992).

KTFM-FM, 1996 FCC LEXIS 6238 (1996).

KUPD-FM, 1997 FCC LEXIS 7041 (1997).

Report on the Broadcast of Violent, Indecent, and Obscene Material, 32 Rad. Reg.2d 1367 (1973).

WBZU-FM, 11 FCC Rcd 13214 (1996).

WCMF-AM & FM, 12 FCC Rcd 8282 (1997).

WEBN-FM, 1997 FCC LEXIS 3207 (1997).

WEZB-FM, 12 FCC Rcd 4147 (1997).

WFBQ-FM, 6 FCC Rcd 3692 (1990).

WFXR-TV, 12 FCC Rcd 8277 (1997).

WGRF-FM, 10 FCC Rcd 5149 (1995).

WIOD-AM, 6 FCC Rcd 3704 (1989).

WLLZ-FM, 6 FCC Rcd 3698 (1989).

WLUP-AM, 6 FCC Rcd 3708 (1989).

WLUP-AM, 8 FCC Rcd 1266 (1993).

WSUC-FM, 8 FCC Rcd 456 (1993).

WVIC-FM, 6 FCC Rcd 2178 (1991).

WVIC-FM, 11 FCC Rcd 12744 (1996).

WWST-FM, 9 FCC Rcd 4871 (1994).

WWWE-AM, 6 FCC Rcd 3711 (1990)

WXRK-FM, 12 FCC Rcd 8274 (1997).

WXRK-FM, WYSP-FM, and WJFK-FM, 5 FCC Rcd 7291 (1990).

WXRK-FM, WYSP-FM, and WJFK-FM, 8 FCC Rcd 2688 (1992).

WXRK-FM, WYSP-FM, WJFK-FM and WJFK-AM, 8 FCC Rcd 6740 (1993).

WXRK-FM, WYSP-FM, WJFK-FM and WJFK-AM, 9 FCC Rcd 1746 (1994).

WXRK-FM, WYSP-FM, WJFK-FM and WJFK-AM, 9 FCC Rcd 6442 (1994).

WYBB-FM, 7 FCC Rcd 1595 (1992).

WZTA-FM, 6 FCC Rcd 3702 (1989).

Congressional Documents

Hearings Before the Committee on Commerce, Science, and Transportation, United States Senate, Alfred C. Sikes, Sherrie P. Marshall, and Andrew C. Barrett, To Be Commissioners, Federal Communications Commission, 101st Cong.,1st. Sess. 392-495 (1989).

Court Cases

Action for Children's Television v. FCC (ACT I), 852 F.2d 1332 (D.C. Cir. 1988).

Action for Children's Television v. FCC (ACT II), 932 F.2d 1504 (D.C. Cir. 1991).

Action for Children's Television v. FCC (ACT III), 11 F.3d 170 (D.C. Cir. 1993).

Action for Children's Television v. FCC (ACT III, *en banc rehearing*), No. 93-1092. (D.C. Cir. 1995).

FCC v. Pacifica Foundation, 438 U.S. 726 (1978).

Illinois Citizens Committee for Broadcasting v. FCC, 41 FCC.2d 777 (1973).

Miller v. California, 413 U.S. 1 (1973)

Pacifica Foundation v. FCC, 556 F.2d 9 (1977).

Robinson v. FCC, 334 F.2d 534 (1964).

Index

7-Eleven, 74
Absolute Strangers, 77, 135
ACLU, 37, 43, 45
ACT I, 51, 53, 54, 55, 99, 155
ACT II, 53, 54, 55, 99, 155
ACT III, 54, 155
ACT III, en banc rehearing, 155
Action for Children's Television, 50, 51, 155
AFA Journal, 73, 75, 88, 89, 90
American Family Association, 1, 2, 4, 6, 7, 7, 9,10, 11, 35, 62, 63, 71, 72, 73, 74, 75, 76, 77, 78, 79, 80, 81, 82, 85, 86, 87, 88, 89, 90, 91, 92, 93, 94, 95, 98, 99, 101, 102, 103, 104, 105, 106, 108, 109, 110, 111, 113, 114, 115, 116, 118, 119, 120, 121, 122, 123, 124, 125, 126, 127, 146
April (1987) Trio, 17, 49, 51, 55, 69, 70, 75, 80, 82, 86, 94, 96, 97, 114, 116, 119, 141, 142
Backwell, Morton, 65
Barrett, Andrew, 93, 107, 108, 109, 111, 118, 122, 123, 125, 155
Blockbuster Music, 75
"Bloom County," 77, 130
Boy Scouts, 78
"Brooklyn South," 76
Burch, Dean, 43, 107
Byrd, Robert, 53, 54, 105
Calvin Klein Ads, 67, 148
Carlin, George, 41, 43, 44, 47, 48, 61, 68, 69, 86, 113, 114, 131, 148
Carson, Johnny, 71
Charren, 71
Christian Leaders for Responsible Television, 9, 73
Coalition for Better Television, 9, 73, 76
Coleman, Peggy, 109, 122, 123
Congress, 4, 6, 8, 15, 23, 25, 29, 45, 52, 54, 55, 59, 65, 70, 79, 85, 100, 106, 111, 112, 122, 123, 124, 127
Cook-Inlet Station Group, 57, 58, 93, 94, 117
Cox, Kenneth, 39, 41, 72, 73, 107, 132
Curl, Brad, 97
"CYCLE II," 42
Dennis, Patricia Diaz, 50, 67, 68, 69, 70, 71, 72, 80, 95, 107, 109, 120, 141, 143
Docket 89-494, 9, 99, 100, 101, 102, 120
Docket 92-223, 9, 105, 122
Douglas, John, 44, 68, 114
Eastern Education Radio, 42, 44
Elders, Jocelyn, 79
"Ellen," 67, 76, 78, 137, 148
Falwell, Jerry, 73
FCC v. Pacifica, 5, 18, 155
Federal Communications Commission, 1, 2, 3, 4, 5, 6, 7, 8,

9, 10, 11, 13, 14, 15, 16, 17, 18, 19, 20, 21, 22, 23, 24, 25, 26, 27, 28, 30, 31, 32, 33, 35, 36, 37, 38, 39, 40, 41, 42, 43, 44, 45, 46, 47, 48, 49, 50, 51, 52, 53, 54, 55, 56, 57, 58, 59, 60, 61, 68, 69, 70, 71, 80, 81, 82, 83, 85, 86, 87, 88, 89, 90, 91, 92, 93, 94, 95, 96, 97, 98, 99, 100, 101, 102, 103, 104, 105, 106, 107, 109, 110, 111, 113, 112, 114, 115, 116, 117, 118, 119, 120, 121, 122, 123, 125, 126, 127, 129, 130, 132, 133, 134, 135, 136, 137, 138, 139, 141, 142, 143, 144, 145, 147, 148, 149, 150, 151, 152, 153, 154, 155
"Femme Forum," 43
First Amendment, 1, 5, 13, 14, 15, 19, 23, 38, 42, 47, 53, 60, 70, 75, 100, 118 133, 139, 144
Fowler, Mark, 10, 48, 49, 70, 95, 96, 97, 107, 109, 116, 119, 124, 135, 139
Freddy Krueger, 78
Garbage Pail Kids, 78
Garcia, Jerry, 42, 61
Gore, Albert 108, 110, 122
Gorman, Paul, 44
Helms, Jesse 51, 52, 53, 54, 70, 89
Hill, Father Morton A., 63, 64, 65, 144
Hollings, Ernest, 108
"Howard Stern Show," 52, 57, 58, 86, 87, 111, 113, 114, 115, 150
Hundt, Reed, 11, 35, 60, 107, 108
Illinois Citizens Committee for Broadcasting, 43, 155
Illinois Citizens Committee for Broadcasting v. FCC, 44, 155
Indecency, 1, 2 3, 4, 5, 6, 7, 9, 13, 15, 16, 17, 18, 19, 20, 21, 22, 23, 32, 33, 35, 36, 37, 42, 43, 44, 45, 46, 47, 48, 49, 51, 53, 54, 55, 56, 57, 58, 59, 60, 61, 68, 69, 70, 71, 80, 82, 85, 86, 92, 93, 94, 95, 96, 99, 100, 102, 103, 104, 105, 106, 107, 108, 109, 110, 115, 116, 117, 118, 119, 121, 122, 129, 130, 132, 133, 134, 135, 136, 137, 138, 140, 141, 142, 144, 145, 146, 148, 149, 150, 151, 152
Infinity Broadcasting, 49, 52, 55, 57, 58, 59, 60, 61, 80, 81, 82, 86, 89, 93, 94, 96, 116, 117, 118, 122, 134, 137, 148, 152
Inouye, Daniel, 54
Jack Straw Memorial Foundation, 40, 60, 151
<u>Jerker</u>, 49, 52, 69, 148
"Jerry Springer," 67
Johnson, Lyndon, 64, 107
Karmazin, Mel, 59
Kasten, Bob, 108
KCSB, 49, 55
Keeley, Mary, 86, 96, 114
KFBI, 58
KLSX, 57, 58
Kmart, 75, 143
KPFK, 39
KRAB, 41
Krasnow, Longley, and Terry's <u>The Politics of Broadcast Regulation</u>, 1, 2, 3, 4, 8, 11, 13, 23, 24, 28, 29, 30, 31, 32, 33, 112, 113, 123, 124, 125, 126, 127, 138, 139
KRTH, 94, 117
KZKC, 55, 81
Last Temptation of Christ, The, 77
Levi Strauss, 78
Liles, Allen, 74
Linker, Winfrey, 26, 65, 140
<u>Lolita</u>, 67, 143

"Love, Sidney," 76, 77, 146
"Lunchpail," 44, 45
"Makin' Bacon," 49
Marilyn Manson, 77
Marshall, Sherrie, 107, 108, 109, 111, 118, 122, 123, 125, 155
"Masterpiece Theatre," 92
McAteer, Ed, 109
McGeady, Paul, 68, 70, 97, 105
"Mighty Mouse," 78, 150
Milam, Lorenzo, 40
Miller v. California, 5, 46, 67, 142, 155
Minow, Newton, 71, 107
"Miss America," 77
Moore, Ray, 109
Moral Majority, 73
Morality in Media, 1, 2, 4, 6, 7, 9, 10, 11, 35, 44, 48, 62, 63, 64, 65, 66, 67, 68, 69, 70, 71, 82, 85, 86, 87, 91, 92, 93, 94, 95, 96, 97, 98, 99, 100, 101, 103, 104, 105, 106, 109, 111, 113, 114, 115, 116, 117, 119, 120, 121, 122, 123, 124, 125, 126, 129, 131, 143, 145
"Murphy Brown," 76, 129
National Decency Forum, 95, 97
National Endowment for the Arts, 79
National Federation of Decency, 72
National Obscenity Law Center, 65, 142
Nightmare on Elm Street, 78
"NYPD Blue," 76, 133
Obscenity, 5, 18, 20, 21, 45, 53, 64, 66, 67, 68, 69, 79, 135, 137, 138, 141, 143, 148, 149, 151
Occupation, Foole, 44
Operation Yorkville, 64
Pacifica Foundation, 1, 18, 19, 23, 38, 39, 44, 45, 46, 47, 48, 49, 50, 52, 55, 60, 61, 68, 69, 86, 92, 100, 102, 105, 114, 117, 129, 130, 138, 149, 151, 152, 155
Pacifica Foundation v. FCC, 46, 155
Paley, William, 71
Palmetto Broadcasting, 11, 14, 36, 38, 60, 109, 151
Palmetto Family Caucus, 109
Patrick, Dennis, 95, 107, 109, 120, 138, 139
Penthouse, 74
Peters, Robert, 68, 143
Playboy, 74, 75, 136, 146
Pornography Awareness Week, 66
Priest, 77, 148
Private Lessons, 55
Profanity, 6
Quello, James, 57, 58, 70, 88, 93, 107, 108, 117
"Quillo" Mispelling, 88, 89, 90, 114
Reagan, Ronald, 48, 53, 65, 95, 120, 137, 144
Reilly, Joseph, 71, 144
Religious Roundtable, 109
"Report on the Broadcast of Violent, Indecent, and Obscene Material," 45, 154
"Ricki Lake," 67
Robinson, Edward, 36, 37, 151, 155
Robinson v. FCC, 37, 155
Rockefeller, John D., 110
Rose, The, 96
Safe Harbor, 19, 51, 133, 138, 148
"Saturday Night Live," 76
Sawyer, Paul, 40
Sikes, Alfred, 10, 56, 107, 108, 109, 110, 111, 117, 118, 122, 123, 125, 133, 155
Smith, Jack, 10, 96, 97, 120
Sonderling Broadcasting, 19, 42, 43, 44, 61, 153
Southland Corporation, 74

Stern, Howard, 2, 19, 50, 56, 57, 58, 59, 61, 70, 71, 76, 77, 78, 80, 81, 87, 88, 90, 91, 93, 94, 96, 113, 114, 115, 117, 118, 119, 129, 132, 134, 136, 137, 141, 147, 148, 150
Stevens, John Paul, 47
Supreme Court, 1, 5, 18, 19, 20, 23, 36, 44, 47, 48, 52, 61, 69, 100, 103, 114, 130
"Topless Radio," 14, 15, 43, 61, 131
Turn Off the TV Day, 67
U.S. Court of Appeals for the District of Columbia, 37, 46, 54, 47, 51, 99
"Vegetable Report," 46
Waldenbooks, 75
"Walk with an Erection," 56
Walker, Charlie, 14, 36, 37, 60, 147
Walt Disney, 78
WBAI, 18, 39, 44, 45, 86, 152
WDKD, 36
Westcott, Al, 81, 115
WEZB, 91, 92
WGBH, 48, 69, 92, 93, 117, 152
White House, 4, 65, 96, 124, 127
White Ribbons Against Pornography, 66
Wildmon, Donald, 9, 71, 72, 73, 75, 76, 77, 78, 79, 80, 81, 87, 95, 96, 97, 109, 114, 118, 119, 130, 132, 138, 139, 142, 143, 146, 149
WJFK, 57, 150
WLLZ, 56
WUHY, 42, 43
WXRK, 71, 80, 87, 88, 89, 90, 91, 144
WYSP, 87, 88

MELLEN STUDIES IN JOURNALISM

1. John L. Morris, **A Study of Attitudes Toward Audience Interaction in Journalism: Citizen-Based Reporting**
2. Joseph C. Manzella, **The Struggle to Revitalize American Newspapers**
3. Kimberly Zarkin, **Anti-Indecency Groups and the Federal Communications Commission: A Study in the Politics of Broadcast Regulations**
4. Raymond N. Ankney, **The Influence of Communication Technologies on Political Participation and Social Interaction**